The Faith That Saves:
The Nature of Faith in the New Testament

An Exegetical and Theological Analysis of the Nature of New Testament Faith

---

Fred Chay, Ph.D.
John P. Correia, M.Div.

WIPF & STOCK · Eugene, Oregon

Wipf and Stock Publishers
199 W 8th Ave, Suite 3
Eugene, OR 97401

The Faith That Saves
The Nature of Faith in the New Testament - An Exegetical and Theological Analysis
 on the Nature of New Testament Faith
By Chay, Fred and Correia, John P.
Copyright©2008 Grace Line Inc
ISBN 13: 978-1-62032-417-2
Publication date 7/15/2012
Previously published by Schoettle Publishing Co, 2008

The Faith That Saves: The Nature of Faith in the New Testament

There is no more important issue in theological study than the meaning of Faith in the New Testament. The perennial problem of the misunderstanding concerning the nature of faith has produced a variety of theological errors as well as pastoral problems for the church. In a day of rampant theological confusion concerning justification by faith the nature of faith is paramount. This book provides a penetrating examination through exegetical precision, concerning the nature of faith. For those who believe in "faith alone in Christ alone" this book will guide you into an understanding of what faith is and what it is not. This is a book that needed to be written and a book that must be read.

> Earl Radmacher, Th.D.
> President Emeritus, Western Seminary

In the great conversation of all things salvific, the jailer's words, "What must I do to be saved?" have continued to shape biblical discussions. One would think his answer, "believe…" would have been enough. Believing, however, has come under much scrutiny and confusion because of theological assumptions and sloppy interpretive methods.

Chay and Correia insist that good scholarship, sound methodology, and a little common sense will birth clarity out of confusion. Through an intense and detailed consideration of the "nature of Faith," the authors show that the scriptures present faith with a profound simplicity that maintains room for a child to receive and a scholar to research.

So, what is faith? Take time with this work--- I believe you'll be persuaded that the simplicity of the author's proposal will part the waters of confusion.

> Fred Lybrand, D.Min.
> Senior Pastor , Northeast Bible Church
> San Antonio, Texas

"Oh, what a find! A book for any person who has wrestled with the nature of New Testament faith. Every teacher or student of biblical theology will be forever indebted to Chay and Correia. They hoped that this book would help its readers gain a sense of what the many thinkers of the past and present have had to say about faith and evaluated their methodology and found many of them wanting. They have asked the tough question which needs to be always asked—I see your answer, now show me how you arrived at that. Chay & Correia state their goal as follows:

> *"It appears that in the sea of theology many a theologian has found their ship broken up upon an a priori commitment to a theological system. It is our goal to 'sail the center of the passage,' so to speak, and arrive at a biblical model of faith that is consistent with the lexical, grammatical, syntactical and contextual evidence provided by the Scriptures."*

They have achieved their goal with "distinction." The Christian community, especially those who understand the biblical teachings of the freeness of God's grace, is clearly indebted to Chay and Correia for providing a clear, accurate, and readable text on the Nature of New Testament Faith in a refreshingly relevant way for our day.

> Stephen R. Lewis, Ph.D.
> President, Rocky Mountain Bible College,
> Rocky Mountain Seminary
> Denver, Colorado

Dedication

This book is dedicated to three men who have impacted my life through
manifesting their commitment to the Lord Jesus Christ
and modeling their skills as my teachers.

Zane Hodges who conferred to me the skill and joy of exegesis
Charles C. Ryrie who challenged me to be a theologian
Norm Geisler who compelled me to be an apologist

I am forever grateful,
Fred Chay

To my wife, Laura, whose love never ceases to amaze me
To Keith Krell, who led me to Christ and leads me in Him
To Dr. F. Olden Pittman, who instilled in me a love for
God's Word
John Correia.

Contents

Index of Charts and Figures

Introduction

"Faith" is a Rorschach word. Define it and you immediately say something about yourself and your theology. It is a term laypeople, pastors and professors frequently use without fully appreciating its meaning or the manner in which the meaning was ascertained. As evangelicals we hold to the full and complete infallibility, inspiration and inerrancy of the sacred Scriptures. With this in mind, the precise meaning of the words contained in Scripture is vital, since they are the very words of God.[1] Faith is chief among the words that demand precision in meaning, occupying such a central role in biblical theology.

The study of language has made significant advancement since James Barr rightfully blasted the academy for its impoverished methodology and misunderstanding concerning lexical study.[2] The recent resurgence of interest in language study (and the correction of methodological errors) has been a windfall for biblical studies and theological inquiry. Linguistics is concerned with the formal study of language, and since the Bible is written in human languages (three, in fact) it is vitally important to understand and appreciate linguistics.

Semantics and lexicography have to do with the meaning of symbols and words. The dependency upon diachronic lexical studies has been supplemented if not supplanted by the need of synchronic lexical analysis.[3]

---

[1] This is in reference to the original or the autographs of the scriptures. It does not include translations nor any extant Greek or Hebrew text we possess. We ascribe to the Chicago Statement of Inerrancy.

[2] See James Barr, *The Semantics of Biblical Language* (London, Oxford University Press, 1961) for the seminal discussion in the mid-20th century that corrected and lambasted many methodological and exegetical errors.

[3] If the context of words change then the content of a word may change. Diachronic lexical analysis traces the development of word meaning over time, while synchronic analysis evaluates a word within a limited time period and largely ignores historical antecedents. Synchronic analysis is more concerned with the context of usage (such as analyzing the word in a given passage, a given book, and a given author), while diachronic analysis is more interested in tracing the development of a word through the history of revelation. Both are useful; however, an overdependence upon diachronic analysis can lead the exegete to depend heavily on a reference that is far removed in time from a biblical usage. The problem in this methodology

The blossoming fields of semantics, linguistics and Discourse Analysis have provided a rich field of inquiry for biblical studies and biblical theology. These gains can only help us as we seek to study the biblical text and from it build soundly biblical theology.

Text and theology must operate and collaborate in the process of biblical interpretation. However, the latter must develop from the former; else our theology has no hope of maintaining a link to the intent of the authors of Scripture. Nevertheless, theologians at all levels of training and skill, from new believers and lay leaders to pastors and professors, are frequently blinded by pre-understanding or bias which prevents the proper functioning of the hermeneutical spiral.[4]

The Reformation, preceded and aided by the faithfulness of both John Huss and John Wycliffe, unshackled the church from the stranglehold of the Roman Catholic Church by reexamining the doctrine of salvation by faith alone in Christ alone. *Sola Fide* was the battle cry across Europe, and later spread from there across the remainder of the known world. However, today it appears to be as Lenin declared in his book *One Step Forward, Two Steps Back.* The gains of the Reformation have been mitigated or at least profoundly abridged by a new working definition of "saving faith." This

---

can readily be seen in the development of the English language in the last 400 or even 200 years. Few modern readers understand Elizabethan usage (Shakespeare being the prime example). Even reading Abraham Lincoln's Emancipation Proclamation, with it's opening "Fourscore and seven years ago…" gives the reader an understanding of how language changes over relatively short time spans. The same is true of the biblical languages, which means the biblical scholar must be careful in diachronic analysis not to bring a usage that is too ancient or too far past the usage they are considering.

[4] The "Hermeneutical spiral" is a spin-off of the Hermeneutical Circle and a proposed solution to the problem of maintaining the distinction between objective textual Meaning and its Significance for the interpreter, yet at the same time uniting both aspects in the interpretive process. The interpreter approaches the text with his or her own pre-understanding and questions for the purpose of determining its meaning. There is a fusion of horizons and the interpreter's pre-understanding is adjusted by the answers given in this exchange. When the interpreter next approaches the text, their pre-understanding is different and so the questions put to the text will be modified. The process is continuous and spirals toward a more and more complete and accurate interpretation of the text. See *The Dictionary of Hermeneutics*, (Gospel Publishing House, 2005).

definition has been introduced, inculcated, and instructed by "theological dogmatics" without legitimate exegetical foundation.[5]

The purpose of this study is to analyze and critically evaluate certain aspects of methodology in handling the linguistic evidence concerning the nature of faith in the New Testament. Further, we will examine and critique the convoluted results of improper methodology often evidenced in theological discussion. The study concerning the philosophy of and philology in religion has revealed that religious language often displays a special semantic development. This is true with the biblical word group for "faith" or "belief," both in Hebrew and Greek. However, it seems that the overlap of concepts imported from not only linguistic studies but also prior theological commitments have produced a hazard to biblical evangelical theology. As Aristotle warned, "The least initial deviation from the truth is later multiplied a thousand fold."

The ancient mariners, according to Greek mythology, had their navigational skills tested as they sought to navigate the narrow passage of water between Scylla and Charybdis. Many a vessel found itself wrecked upon the rock of Scylla and sucked down into the whirlpool of Charybdis. It appears that in the sea of theology many a theologian has found their ship broken up upon an *a priori* commitment to a theological system. It is the goal of this study to "sail the center of the passage," so to speak, and arrive at a biblical model of faith that is consistent with the lexical, grammatical, syntactical, and contextual evidence provided by the Scriptures.

The eternal destiny of millions of men and women who bear the image of God upon their beings is at stake. Richard Weaver was never more clearheaded when he said in his book of the same title, the truth that "Ideas have Consequences." The idea of "the nature of faith", both its meaning and resultant theology has tremendous consequences.

---

[5] See Fred Chay, "The Danger of Neo Legalism: An Assessment of the Theology of Norman Shepherd, Daniel Fuller, John Piper, Thomas Schreiner, and Paul Rainbow Concerning the Nature of Faith"

Πίστις and its verbal derivative πιστεύω are the Greek words that will be of major concern to us as we seek to examine the biblical evidence for the nature of faith. The relation of these two words to each other and their use in different contexts is the *crux interpretum*. The root of the two words is also a serious issue that merits considerable analysis and discussion.

There are five main sections to this study that fit into a composite whole from which to derive answers.

1. Theological Consensus – Contemporary Christian authors and scholars will be discussed. The effect of their view of faith on soteriology will also be examined.
2. Lexicography – The major lexicons will be consulted for word analysis and study of function. Word study methodology will also be discussed to consider pitfalls, proper use and results.
3. Syntactical Issues – The use of πιστεύω with various Greek prepositions will be examined, and the impact of the various prepositions on translation and exegesis will be discussed.
4. Grammatical Issues – Verbal grammar usage with various tenses will be considered for their affect on our understanding of the nature of faith.
5. Textual Usage – Consideration of various major Scripture passages related to faith/belief will be examined in light of the preceding study.

The goal of the procedure outlined above is to follow proper procedure within a literal-grammatical-historical hermeneutic, to evaluate the biblical evidence regarding the nature of faith, and then to align our theology with the biblical evidence. Faith is indeed a Rorschach word, and our definition gives insight into our entire theological grid. With this in mind, we must be exceedingly vigilant to seek the definition of faith that most closely aligns with the biblical evidence.

Theological Consensus

It is useful as we begin our study to assess the current state of the debate among respected evangelical scholars. There has been much ink spilled on this topic, and the sides are well-entrenched. Any military general will first seek to assess the condition of the battlefield before deciding upon tactics, and it is not far from the truth to describe the state of affairs over the nature of faith as a battle. Thus we begin by assessing the battlefield.

The predominant view in the world of evangelicalism is that faith is not only an acknowledgement that the statements of the Bible are true. True faith, it is argued, involves obedience to the commands of the Savior in whom faith is placed. The argument claims lexical and grammatical support from the Greek text of the New Testament. While this is not an ancient belief, it is not completely new either. Consider the theologically laced comment of Rudolph Bultmann:

> πίστις is the "oath of fidelity," "the pledge of faithfulness," "security." This leads on the one side to the sense of "certainty," "trustworthiness," on the other to that of "means of proof," "proof." In particular πίστις denotes the reliability of persons, "faithfulness." It belongs esp. to friendship (φιλία).[6]

This is quoted from *The Theological Dictionary of the New Testament*, edited by Gerhard Kittel. Although TDNT has been lambasted for poor methodology[7] and is a theological dictionary and not a lexicon, it is used by many today as a *de facto* lexicon without critical reflection or consideration as to its biases and shortcomings. Notice the phraseology: an "oath of

---

[6] Rudolph Bultmann, "πίστις" in Gerhard Kittel, Geoffrey William Bromley, and Gerhard Friedrich, eds., *The Theological Dictionary of the New Testament* (Grand Rapids, MI; Eerdmans, 1964-1976), Vol. 6, Page 177; hereafter referred to as TDNT.
[7] See James Barr, *Semantics of Biblical Languages*, and D.A. Carson, *Exegetical Fallacies*, 2nd ed. (Baker Book House, 1996). Also see, Robert D. Preus, "Perennial Problems in the Doctrine of Justification". Concordia Theological Monthly. July, 1981, pp. 163-183.

fidelity," and the fact that it is a "means of proof." These statements are offered by Bultmann without support, but many students miss this fact and accept his conclusions. This can only lead to the exegetical error of eisegesis in place of exegesis, the bane of every evangelical scholar.

One of the most famous proponents of the *working faith* view is Dr. John F. MacArthur. Being the pastor of one of the nation's larger churches and chancellor of Master's Seminary has given him a place of prominence, and his book debate with Zane Hodges has gained him a large and devoted audience. This issue is addressed in his books *The Gospel According to Jesus*, and *Faith Works: The Gospel According to the Apostles*. In chapter three of the latter title, MacArthur analyzes several Greek words, notably for this study πίστις and πιστεύω. It is important to realize that MacArthur sees his opponents to be creating an absolute parallel between the Greek words and the English words in question.

> "Let's suppose that *faith* and *believe* are satisfactory
> equivalents of the Greek words *pistis* ("faith, faithfulness")
> and *pisteuo* ("to believe, entrust"). What do English
> dictionaries say about faith?"[8]

MacArthur goes on to cite numerous definitions of "faith" and "believe" from two well known and highly regarded English dictionaries, including a definition of "loyalty" which solidifies his point. He makes this argument under the assumption that English-Greek equivalence is a fundamental part of the arguments of opponents to Lordship salvation.[9] Another consideration is MacArthur's uses the two Greek words under consideration here with nothing else said regarding the usage of those Greek words in the ancient Greek language. It can be supposed that he wants the book to appeal to a general audience, but we must be careful in taking our word analysis too lightly regardless of our intended readers.

---

[8] John F. MacArthur, *Faith Works: The Gospel According to the Apostles.* (Grand Rapids, MI; Word Publishing, 1993), 38

[9] Ibid. See Fred Chay, *Lordship Salvation as Taught by John MacArthur* (Th.M. thesis; Dallas Theological Seminary, 1983) for a rebuttal.

In order to expand the general consensus even further, while not leaving the discussion of the study of New Testament words, it is important to realize that the majority of teachers and scholars impassioned in this debate focus on the progression of saving faith. This is done by utilizing three major categories, in which each one builds upon the prior. Those categories are *notitia* (knowledge), *assensus* (intellectual acceptance), and *fiducia* (trust/obedience). Wayne Grudem, in his *Systematic Theology*, uses the English word equivalents (knowledge, approval, and personal trust).[10] Grudem states clearly that the first two are insufficient to provide eternal deliverance, and only when combined with the third (personal, volitional trust) can a person be granted eternal life with God. The first two are generally agreed upon within evangelicalism, but the third is where some dispute arises depending on the articulation of *fiducia* by the individual scholar. Gordon Clark, a staunchly Reformed scholar, makes a salient point regarding the articulation of this three-fold formula:

> ...What does it mean to believe? The question is usually asked in Latin rather than in Greek, and so phrased the question becomes, What is faith? Various theologians have offered psychological analyses of faith. The most common Protestant analysis is that *fides* is a combination of *notitia, assensus*, and *fiducia*. If these last three Latin words can be explained, then one may compare *fides* and *pistis* or *pisteuoo* to see if they are synonymous. If these Latin terms cannot be defined, then they do not constitute an analysis of faith.[11]

Clark then goes on to define *notitia* as intellectual content known[12], and *assensus* as one's voluntary acceptance of a proposition.[13] Clark explains that this assent is not merely intellectual; assent primarily involves the volition or will. He states, "...belief is definitely intellectual and volitional. The good news, *i.e.*, information, must be understood and assented to. This

---

[10] See Wayne Grudem, *Systematic Theology* (Grand Rapids, MI; Zondervan, 1994, 2000), 709-12
[11] Gordon Clark, *What is Saving Faith?* (n.p.; The Trinity Foundation, 1990), 146
[12] Ibid, 146-47
[13] Ibid, 147

is belief."[14] Seen in this way, *assensus* is not a passive agreement that facts are true; rather, it is an active, volitional decision wherein the will controls the intellect and agrees with the knowledge gained. Lastly, concerning *fiducia*, Clark states, "... the term *fiducia*, which today is often confidently joined with knowledge and assent to make the definition of faith, has never been unambiguously explained."[15] Any scholar would recognize the typical Reformed presentation of *fiducia* as an act of trust as being part of initial faith in Christ, but as Clark has argued this initial volitional decision is included in *assensus* and is therefore redundant in discussion of *fiducia*. The real problem arises as the word *fiducia* has additional meaning, such as obedience or ongoing commitment, added to it. This is also the case with Greek terminology. As Augustine puts it with regard to saving faith,

> ...it is yet necessary that everything which is believed
> should be believed after thought has preceded; although
> even belief itself is nothing else than to think with assent.[16]

Kim Riddlebarger wrote on the difference between Zane Hodges' and John MacArthur's views on the content of saving faith, and in the end his analysis is as follows:

> Faith defined as mere assent is nothing of which
> demons are not capable. Faith must be something more
> than Hodges' definition of simply believing the truth of the
> propositions of Scripture. Faith must be directly connected
> to repentance in some sense, and someone who exercises
> the kind of faith that saves must submit to Christ's
> authority as Lord.[17]

Frank Thielman presents faith in these terms:

> "Faith" as mere intellectual assent to various
> propositions, however, is worthless for salvation or
> justification, and saving faith is more than simply an entry

---

[14] Ibid, 156

[15] Ibid, 150

[16] Philip Schaff, *The Nicene and Post-Nicene Fathers Vol. V*, (Saint Augustin: Anti-Pelagian Writings.; Oak Harbor: Logos Research Systems, 1997), 499.

[17] Kim Riddlebarger, "What is Faith?" in Michel Horton, ed., *Christ the Lord: The Reformation and Lordship Salvation* (Grand Rapids, MI; Baker Books, 1992), 95

point to the people of God. The command of God that we must obey, says the Elder, is not only to "believe in the name of his Son, Jesus Christ," but also "to love one another" (1 John 3:23). Even faith that can move mountains, says Paul, has no benefit without love (1 Cor. 13:2), and faith implies obedience (Rom. 1:5; 16:26). As James points out, faith without works is dead (James 2:26).

Faith, therefore, is not primarily acknowledgement of a body of doctrine but a conviction about the truth of the gospel so strong that it radically reorients one's life toward dependence on God even in the most difficult circumstance.[18]

It remains to be analyzed and decided whether a concept of obedience or personal dedication to holiness is included in the definition of faith in the New Testament. We must analyze the texts, the words, and the scholarly input to determine if obedience or ongoing commitment is an essential component of salvific faith.

R.H. Stein makes this statement concerning saving faith in his commentary on Luke in the *New American Commentary* series:

How does one share in God's gracious offer of salvation? What response is demanded by God's initiative in offering salvation to humanity? In Luke-Acts this also is expressed in various ways. One of the most frequent descriptions of the necessary response is "to believe." This is clearly seen in Acts 16:31, where the question "What must I do to be saved?" in 16:30 is answered, "Believe in the Lord Jesus, and you will be saved." The offer of salvation requires the human response of faith. A second response frequently emphasized is the need for repentance. One receives salvation by repenting. This repentance can be expressed in specific ways, such as selling one's possessions and giving to the poor (16:9; 18:22; 19:8–10) or bearing fruit befitting repentance (3:8; Acts 26:20). The need for baptism is also frequently associated with the human response, which results in salvation. Sometimes the needed response is said to be confessing Christ (9:26; 12:8–9; Acts 22:16; cf. Rom 10:9), taking up a cross (Luke 9:23; 14:27), following Jesus (9:23, 57–62), keeping the

---

[18] Frank Thielman, *Theology of the New Testament* (Grand Rapids, MI; Zondervan, 2005) ,694-95

commandments (10:25–28; 18:18–20), hearing and
keeping God's word (11:28), or being obedient to God
(Acts 5:31–32; 10:35).

    Clearly these are not to be understood as different ways
of acquiring salvation. Rather they are various ways of
expressing *the* needed human response to God's offer of
salvation. All the above are part of *the* response God
demands. Disciples do not pick and choose which aspects
of the response they "like." They enter into God's
kingdom through *one* response that involves faith,
repentance, baptism, confessing Christ, following Jesus,
and keeping the commandments. This does not mean that
entrance into salvation is a process. Rather entrance into
salvation involves that indivisible act in which all these
responses are contained; for true faith includes repentance,
the willingness to be baptized, and obedience.[19] (emphasis
original)

Stein's above argument speaks to the heart of the issue. Is "faith" to be

equated with baptism, confession, following Jesus, and keeping His

commandments? Are all of these ideas contained within the meaning of the

words "faith" and "believe"? Reformed theologians argue that the terms are

synonymous, but it remains to be seen if the texts will sustain this thesis.

    One proponent of "working faith" who has articulated this teaching well

is R.C. Sproul.[20] Sproul agrees with MacArthur's doctrinal arguments by

interweaving classical philosophical arguments with them. Surprisingly,

neither one really deals with New Testament Greek on the subject of faith.[21]

The classic Reformed position is boldly assumed by Dr. Sproul as he

articulates the idea of *fiducia* inherent in true saving faith:

---

[19] R.H. Stein, *Luke*, vol. 24 of *The New American Commentary* (Nashville, TN; Broadman &
Holman Publishers; 2001), 50-51. Stein is essentially articulating the position of James D.G.
Dunn in his book, *Unity and Diversity in the New Testament: An Inquiry into the Character of
Earliest Christianity* (Harrisburg, PA; Trinity Press International, 1999), 258-265, which present
a multifaceted gospel message.

[20] It is important to note that the following quotes are in the context of Dr. Sproul's rebuttal to
the very conciliatory dialogues going on between Evangelicals and Catholics. A consideration
that needs evaluation is the size of the divide between "working faith" and the faith-works
justification of Roman Catholicism, though the ecumenical issue is beyond the scope of this
paper.

[21] Though this is true with these particular quotes, both authors use this basis elsewhere.

"The element of *fiducia* includes a dramatic change in our value system.... For saving faith to occur there must be a real change in the person....This certainly involves a change in emotion, disposition, inclination, and volition."[22]

Dr. Sproul imputes a large amount of inherent meaning into the word. He makes his point even more forcefully in his book *Getting the Gospel Right*:

"Though faith and works can and must be distinguished from one another, they must not be separated. True faith *always necessarily and inevitably* issues in a changed life, made manifest by works."[23]

He further asserts that there must be a trusting reliance as evidenced by good works in his book *Grace Unknown: The Heart of Reformed Theology*:

The presence of both *notitia* and *assensus* is still insufficient for justification. Even the devil has these elements. Satan is aware of the data of the gospel and is more certain of their truth than we are. Yet he hates and despises the truth of Christ. He will not rely on Christ or his righteousness because he is the enemy of Christ. The elements of *notitia* and *assensus* are necessary conditions for justification (we cannot be justified without them), but they are not sufficient conditions. A third element must be present before we possess the faith that justifies.[24]

The vehemence of the statement leads the reader to think that the matter is settled. However, others within the evangelical world differ with advocates for Lordship salvation. Proponents of what is commonly called "Free Grace" represent the other side of the debate over the nature of faith. One of these proponents is Dr. Charles Bing. In his doctoral dissertation for Dallas Theological Seminary, Bing argues against the Lordship salvation proponent's view of faith. Consider this statement:

---

[22] R.C. Sproul, *Faith Alone: The Evangelical Doctrine of Justification*. (Grand Rapids, MI; Baker Book House, 1995), 87

[23] R.C. Sproul, *Getting the Gospel Right*. (Grand Rapids, MI; Baker Book House, 1999), 69 (emphasis mine)

[24] R.C. Sproul, *Grace Unknown: The Heart of Reformed Theology* (Grand Rapids, MI; Baker Book House, 2000), 72. Sproul does not, to our knowledge, evaluate the assumption that demonic soteriology and human soteriology may be unilaterally equated. The Scriptures give us precious little evidence regarding the angelic realm, and speculation is dangerous at best. James 2:19, and its' bearing upon soteriology, is discussed below in the commentary on 2:14-26.

19

"What makes saving faith different from any other faith is its object. Therefore, saving faith is defined as trust or confidence in the Lord Jesus Christ as the Savior from sin. It is a personal acceptance of the work of the Lord Jesus Christ on the cross for the sinner.....When one believes he takes God at His word and personally appropriates the provision of Christ's free gift of salvation for himself."[25]

Proponents of Free Grace such as Bing tend not to point to a difference in the quality of the faith of the individual, but to the object of the faith as salvific or non-salvific. The point of contention between the positions is the person who trusts Jesus as Savior, but not as Lord. Lordship advocates argue that a person who does not trust Jesus as Lord as well as Savior (in the sense of godly sorrow for and forsaking of sin, and obedience to Christ) does not have salvific faith. Dr. David Anderson makes a poignant remark regarding this kind of argument:

"We do not take issue with the assertion that some expressions of faith in the New Testament are not saving faith, that is, do not involve believing salvific content. The notion that in the New Testament believing in Jesus as Savior is not saving faith is simply wrong. The New Testament knows of no sub-level or insufficient faith in Christ as Savior that does not save. Even Simon Magus of Acts 8:13 had saving faith. There is nothing in the text to indicate that his belief and baptism are to be distinguished from the other believers in Samaria."[26]

In reviewing Sproul's *Grace Unknown* and specifically his definition of *fiducia*, Robert Wilkin argues that the redefinition of *fiducia* from "trust" (a synonym for faith) to "characteristic and loving obedience" is misplaced:

How does this view stack up against the Gospel of John? Do we find more than knowledge and assent in the case of the woman at the well and the other Samaritans who came to faith in Christ (John 4)? Where is

---

[25] Charles C. Bing *Lordship Salvation: A Biblical Evaluation and Response.* (Ph.D. diss., Dallas Theological Seminary, 1991), 59. This is primarily an exegetical work dealing with lexical and grammatical issues.
[26] David Anderson, "The Nature of Faith", *Chafer Theological Seminary Journal Volume 5.4* (September 1999), 26. See the discussion below regarding the case of Simon in Acts 8.

commitment indicated in the man born blind (John 9)? Or in the Lord's simple statement to Martha (John 11:25–27)? [*sic*] John's Gospel knows nothing of some third element of saving faith. Indeed the purpose statement of the book says that whoever believes *that* Jesus is the Christ, the Son of God, has everlasting life. Clearly in John nothing more than understanding and acceptance (or assent) are required for eternal life. The same is true in the entire Bible (compare, for example, Gen 15:6 and Rom 4:1–8).[27]

David Anderson goes on in his discussion of the nature of faith in the New Testament and offers this perspective:

No one argues that devotion to Christ and doing good works in His name cannot *point to* faith. They should. However, the *definition* of faith must carefully exclude any *evidence* of faith, because evidences are inherently *inconclusive.* In Matthew 7 does our Lord not reject the false teachers as unbelievers, despite their many good works performed in His name? Although *faith* may produce *obedience,* never does *obedience* produce *faith.* For these reasons, obedience cannot be made a part of faith.[28]

Our view of salvation, i.e. its content and ground, is greatly affected by our view of the nature of faith. It is readily apparent that the issue is firmly divided, and that both sides have capable and committed scholars arguing their case. Having looked at the contemporary thought in both camps, it becomes our duty as Bible students to turn to the Scriptures themselves, examine the lexicons and usages in context, and evaluate the positions to determine which is stronger in light of the evidence. Regardless of our affinity for a trusted and valued theologian, we must be students of the Word and evaluate the positions on their merits to determine which position best represents the teaching of Scripture.

---

[27]Robert Wilkin, "A Review of R.C. Sproul's Grace Unknown: The Heart of Reformed Theology" *Journal of the Grace Evangelical Society volume 14:2* (August 2001), 7
[28] David Anderson, "The Nature of Faith", 12

Lexicography

Our study of the nature of saving faith in the New Testament logically begins with a proper word study. By analyzing the lexical data available on πιστεύω and πίστις, we can begin to build a base from which to gain an understanding of these terms. Only after we have built this foundation can we turn to grammatical and syntactical considerations.

One issue that inevitably comes up when beginning to study the lexicography of a word is the issue of etymology, the study of word origins and roots. The words which are under consideration are initially evaluated by their root. It is interesting to note that Becker, in his discussion of words for faith in the New Testament, put πείθω in as the very first entry.[29] This they base on their conclusion that πιθ is the derivative root of both πείθω and πίστις / πιστεύω.

> The stem *peith-* (*pith-, poith-*) has the basic meaning of trust. The same stem is also the basis of the formations with *pist-* (> pisteuo). Trust can refer to a statement, so that it has the meaning to put faith in, to let oneself be convinced, or to a demand, so that it gets the meaning of obey, be persuaded.[30]

There are some pitfalls here that D.A. Carson highlights summarily. He defines what is called the root fallacy: the presupposition "that every word actually *has* a meaning bound up with its shape or its components."[31] Carson goes on to delineate reasons why lexical students should never use etymology as a determining factor in the meaning of a word. He says "that the meaning of a word cannot be reliably determined by Etymology [sic], or

---

[29] O. Becker, "Faith, Persuade, Belief, Unbelief" in Collin Brown *The New International Dictionary of New Testament Theology.* Volume I. (Grand Rapids MI; Zondervan Publishing House, 1979), 587

[30] Ibid, 588

[31] D. A. Carson, *Exegetical Fallacies,* 28. This error of philology has been brought to the attention of all New Testament exegetes through the work of Barr in *Semantics of Biblical Languages.*

that a root, once discovered, always projects a certain semantic load onto anything that incorporates that root."[32] Alfred Jepsen also cautions, "The meaning of a word cannot be inferred from the (more or less certain) etymology, but only by a careful study of the way it is used in the language."[33] It would seem that in the above entry the root fallacy has been committed, and in the process the semantic range of πείθω has been imported into πιστεύω.

The root fallacy is committed frequently in the debate over belief terminology in the New Testament. As figure 1 illustrates, πιθ is the assumed (and most likely) root word of both πείθω and πίστις. Πείθω has one possible meaning of "to obey." It is assumed that this meaning comes from the literal sense of πιθ which is "to bind." Obey is elaborated in this sense to be a binding of oneself to person for obedience. Some would argue that πίστις is from the same root as πείθω, and therefore they must both carry the same derived meaning. Faith then becomes the binding of oneself in obedience to the object of faith.

If, on the other hand, we heed the cautions above set forth by Carson, we should realize that this theological loading of a word can cause serious trouble. For one thing πείθω is translated into English as "obey" only four times in the New Testament (out of over 50 occurrences). Those occurrences are found in Romans 2:8, Galatians 5:7, Hebrews 13:17, and James 3:3. Secondly, a word study on πείθω shows it to mean convince, persuade, trust, or satisfy (rare). Also, the fact that πίστις is a noun and πείθω is a verb also creates a problem, for then we are loading verbal meaning into a noun. A verb denotes action; a noun has no inherent action.

---

[32] Ibid, 32.

[33] Alfred Jepsen, "אמן" in G. Johannes Botterweck and Helmer Ringgren, eds., *The Theological Dictionary of the Old Testament Vol. 1*, rev. ed., trans. John T. Willis (Grand Rapids, MI; Eerdmans, 1974), 293

One possible exception would be participles, which are both a verb and an adjective, but even still an adjective is not a noun *per se*. An adjective modifies a noun, but is not a noun.[34] To put this in perspective, the noun πίστις is normally translated faith, trust, or confidence. It may or may not have an object.

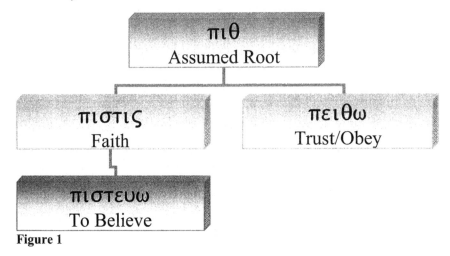

Figure 1

Another of the foremost authorities on the usage of Koine Greek in the New Testament is *A Greek – English Lexicon of the New Testament and other early Christian literature* by Bauer, Arndt, and Gingrich, commonly known as BAG. In an article published in the Journal of the Grace Evangelical Society, Michael Makidon has pointed out some variations in the current update edited by Frederic Danker (referred to as BDAG). Makidon makes this statement at the conclusion of his review of the update:

> "For the most part, those who teach the NT from the
> original language have come to trust Walter Bauer's
> lexical work. Many take the research for granted because

---

[34] This does not ignore the fact that a participle may act substantivally in a sentence and function as a noun equivalent within a contextual setting. A substantival participle is a verbal idea that describes a person, place, or thing so completely that it becomes identified with it, and hence stands as a functional noun equivalent. In a similar manner the devil came to be identified so completely as "the adversary" that his name became, in essence, שָׂטָן (*satan*, "Adversary"). This should not be used to freight verbal ideas into nouns.

of the sweat and toil men have invested in this project over their lifetimes. While much of the research is invaluable, teachers would be well advised to make sure that it corresponds with Scripture before making lasting judgments."[35]

We must carefully examine the reasons for Makidon's critique of BDAG, especially considering the prominent place BDAG enjoys among scholars and pastors. Makidon supports his statement with numerous examples, but one should suffice here to make the point. Consider Figure 2, which shows section two of the definition for πιστεύω (underlining mine):

BAGD – 2ND EDITION

2. *believe* (*in*), *trust* of relig. belief in a special sense, as faith in the Divinity that lays special emphasis on trust in his power and his nearness to help, in addition to being convinced that he exists and that his revelations or disclosures are true. In our lit. God and Christ are objects of this faith.[36]

BDAG – 3RD EDITION

2 **to entrust oneself to an entity in complete confidence, *believe (in)*,** *trust,* w. <u>implication of total commitment to the one who is trusted</u>. In our lit. God and Christ are objects of this type of faith that relies on their power and nearness to help, in addition to being convinced that their revelations or disclosures are true.[37]

Figure 2

---

[35] Michael Makidon, "Soteriological Concerns with Bauer's Greek Lexicon" in *Journal of the Grace Evangelical Society vol 17* (Autumn 2004), 17-18

[36] Arndt, W., Gingrich, F. W., Danker, F. W., & Bauer, W. *A Greek-English lexicon of the New Testament and other early Christian literature : A translation and adaptation of the fourth revised and augmented edition of Walter Bauer's Griechisch-deutsches Worterbuch zu den Schrift en des Neuen Testaments und der ubrigen urchristlichen Literatur* (Chicago: University of Chicago Press, 1979), 661; hereafter referred to as BAGD.

[37] Arndt, W., Danker, F. W., & Bauer, W. *A Greek-English lexicon of the New Testament and other early Christian literature.* "Based on Walter Bauer's Griechisch-deutsches Worterbuch zu den Schriften des Neuen Testaments und der frhüchristlichen [sic] Literatur, sixth edition, ed. Kurt Aland and Barbara Aland, with Viktor Reichmann and on previous English editions by Arndt W., Gingrich F.W., and F.W. Danker." (3rd ed.) (Chicago. University of Chicago Press, 2000), 817; hereafter referred to as BDAG.

Clearly a significant addition was made to the 3rd edition. This begs the question: why was the addition made? Was the additional text added because of better or new textual evidence, or is it possible that the additional commitment and obedience language stems from a new theological presupposition? More will be said about this later on, but at this stage it is worth noting that there appears to be no new evidence given in the 3rd edition to warrant the change. As Eugene Botha warns:

> Perhaps one of the reasons for this unsatisfactory condition today is that the standard works dealing with the meanings of words available to theologians and exegetes are still representative of linguistic and lexicographic theories current at the turn of the century. New editions are just reprints and there is no real change in the basic presuppositions underlying the compilation of such works. A further factor is that traditionally dictionaries are viewed as the only and best sources for meaning and are considered infallible. The user of dictionaries is not aware of the problems in these works and without reserve implements what was found there in exegesis and word studies. This is of course unsatisfactory, because dictionaries can indeed contain serious mistakes.[38]

The lexical evidence, then, seems to have made a recent shift, and in the process committed methodological errors. With this in mind, we must not allow ourselves to stop here; we must continue to study and see if the changes made in the lexica are warranted by the evidence.

The next phase of lexicography is to search out the major lexicons to find all the uses of the word in the New Testament and also in the extra-biblical literature, in particular the Septuagint. It has already been shown the apparent change in BDAG, and so we must be careful when using that source. Basic charts highlighting the occurrences of πιστεύω in the New Testament can be found in Appendix 1.[39]

---

[38] J.E. Botha, "Pisteuo in the Greek New Testament" in *Neotestimentica 21* (1987), 230.

[39] The reader should note that the charts are divided into indicative vs. non-indicative uses. This arrangement will assist in more detailed analysis below.

We must also be very careful when researching the lexical data, as lexicons can and do contain bias (as noted above in BDAG). Botha's article quoted above in *Neotestimentica* is invaluable to the scholar who uses the lexica regularly. He warns of the presence of illegitimate totality transfer present in many lexical entries:

> This [illegitimate totality transfer] is also something which a user of dictionaries must be aware of, for it occurs rather frequently in dictionaries, theological dictionaries, exegesis, and so on. A word is considered to carry more than one meaning in the same context, or to have part of one meaning and part of another simultaneously. Baur's [*sic*] dictionary (1979:661) gives for *pisteuō* "faith…that lays special emphasis on trust…". Obviously the focus here is on "trust", which is one of the meanings for which *pisteuō* can be used. But then he continues and, as part of this meaning, gives "…in addition to being convinced that he exists and that his revelations or disclosures are true". Here another meaning of *pisteuō* is correlated with the first, namely the meaning "to accept something as true". *Pisteuō* cannot mean both these things at the same time. Illegitimate totality transfer has taken place.[40]

One thing that is especially important in this section is to deal with citations from Moulton and Milligan for information regarding usage of the terms in the common era of Greek culture. In Koine πίστις is normally used of faith or confidence in a person. Also, in a passive sense, it can be translated as fidelity or faithfulness.[41] It is also used of a guarantee or pledge, and in some sources of a bond or mortgage.[42] So it seems that πίστις has a wide range of usage, whether with personal encounters or in financial matters.

In the case of πιστεύω it seems that the citations are fairly scarce, although it is clear that it is akin to πίστις, and is simply used to express the

---

[40] J.E. Botha, "Pisteuo in the Greek New Testament", 233-34
[41] J.H. Moulton and G. Milligan. *Vocabulary of the Greek Testament* (Peabody, MA; Hendrickson Publishers, 1997), 515; catalog no. 4102
[42] Ibid.

verbal idea stemming from the noun. Thus Moulton and Milligan make it apparent that the sense in which πιστεύω is used is that of putting faith or trust in something. To believe in something is cited in a few instances.[43] After an exhaustive search of the lexica, Botha found five lexical meanings put forth by the various lexica: "Accept something as correct and truthful"; "to entrust somebody with something"; "to place trust on somebody or something"; and some included "to be a Christian" and "to obey".[44] His analysis of those given ranges after a careful study yielded these conclusions:

> It was found that four of the meanings abstracted from the dictionaries indeed are valid meanings for *pisteuō*. However, a fifth one, "to obey", could not be validated in the New Testament. A careful examination of the dictionaries showed where this notion originated. It was alledged [*sic*] by Van den Ed (1883:1070) and Bartelink (1958:197) on the grounds of the assumed meaning of *pisteuō* in some of the Sophocles tragedies. An examination of these passages revealed that the *implication* of *pisteuō* in those contexts was mistaken for the meaning of *pisteuō*. (The passages under discussion are OedT. 625, OedC. 174 and Trach. 1228f...). This fifth "meaning" of *pisteuō* is thus not an acceptable meaning of *pisteuō*...[45]

Botha's analysis is thorough and reasoned, and bears weight under the scrutiny of the above data. By avoiding the root fallacy as well as the illegitimate totality transfer we can see that lexically the case for obedience being a part of the semantic value of πιστεύω is built upon data that is not strong. Lexically πιστεύω does not include obedience in its semantic range. It remains to be seen whether πιστεύω is used in the New Testament with an *implication* or *contextual* inference of obedience. Here it is simply noted that the *word* does not carry that denotation inherently.

---

[43] Ibid., 514 catalog no. 4100
[44] J.E. Botha, "Pisteuo in the Greek New Testament", 236
[45] Ibid.

In looking at πείθω just briefly, it is clear that in the Koine this word is only used with reference to persuading someone, or being persuaded. It also is used of being obedient.[46] It seems that πείθω has split from πίστις and carries a different semantic force. Every occurrence of πείθω in the New Testament is listed in Appendix 2. In briefly analyzing the occurrences of πείθω in the New Testament it should not escape notice that πείθω is completely unused by John in his Gospel[47], and only occurs once in his Epistles (at 1 John 3:19, where the meaning "persuade" is compelling). The question naturally arises as to whether any supposed interchangeability or overlapping of the semantic range can be maintained in the New Testament in light of this simple fact. John knew the word πείθω, and used it in a manner consistent with the rest of the New Testament. He also completely avoided it in his Gospel, the clearest text we have regarding the expected response to be granted eternal life.

Πιστεύω in the Septuagint[48]

The next essential area of investigation for the student analyzing the meaning of words in the New Testament is the Septuagint. Most if not all of the writers of the New Testament trusted the Septuagint as the version of the Scriptures that they read, studied, and memorized, much as modern American students of Scripture use English translations.[49] And the writers of the New Testament undoubtedly colored, to greater or lesser extents, their

---

[46] Moulton and Milligan, 500 catalog no. 3982

[47] John does use the negative ἀπειθέω at 3:36, which is, according to BDAG, the opposite of the passive of πείθω, i.e. it is listed as the opposite of πείθομαι.

[48] Within this study, when the LXX is mentioned it is readily acknowledged that the LXX was not a monolithic document, but developed over time and use by the Hellenistic Jewish community. Often certainty is elusive as to which recension we are looking at, and especially which edition a given NT writer was utilizing at the time of writing a particular book. For more on the history of the LXX see Karen Jobes and Moises Silva, *Invitation to the Septuagint* (Grand Rapids, MI; Baker Books, 2000). For this study, the work cited is Alfred Rahlfs, *Septuaginta* (Stuttgart; Deutsche Bibelgesellschaft, 1996, c1979).

[49] The majority of quotations and allusions in the Book of Hebrews reveals this, as well as the Book of Revelation. With the exception of the few devoted Pharisees who studied biblical Hebrew, the vast majority of devout Jews read the Septuagint.

theological understanding of terms by their use in the Septuagint. This is no less true with πιστεύω than with any other word.

As a caution, the Septuagint cannot supply all of our answers to the question of the meaning of πιστεύω in the New Testament. Only sound lexical and exegetical methodology, combined with consistent and appropriate hermeneutical controls in detailed study of the New Testament texts themselves can do that. What the Septuagint can offer the scholar, though, is some background on the usage of the term as seen from the eyes of devout Jews living relatively near the time of the writing of the New Testament. As such it is an invaluable tool in the hands of the exegete and insightful into the semantic range of πιστεύω.

Thankfully the study of πιστεύω in the LXX is fairly straightforward. With a single exception (Jeremiah 25:8) every instance of πιστεύω in the LXX stands in place of the Hebrew אָמַן,[50] which greatly simplifies the study. Further assisting the exegete is the fact that πιστεύω overwhelmingly[51] translates the Hiphil stem of אָמַן, again narrowing the focus and the semantic range. The fact that the LXX translators were so selective in using πιστεύω should certainly not escape notice.

Consulting the lexicons for the range of the Hiphil stem of אָמַן is helpful. TWOT lists as the primary denotation of the Hiphil stem "to be certain, i.e. to believe in."[52] Scott goes on to say regarding this term:

> This very important concept in biblical doctrine gives clear evidence of the biblical meaning of "faith" in contradistinction to the many popular concepts of the term.

---

[50] Appendix 3 lists each instance of the term in the LXX, and also considers the few instances where אָמַן occurs in the Hiphil and is translated with something other than πιστεύω in the LXX. In those few instances it is readily noted that compounds of πιστεύω are utilized to bring out some nuance of Hebrew grammar that might otherwise not be apparent to the Greek reader.

[51] Two exceptions, both in the Niphal, are listed in Appendix 1.

[52] Jack Scott, "אָמַן" in R. Laird Harris, Gleason Leonard Archer, and Bruce K. Waltke. *Theological Wordbook of the Old Testament*. (Chicago: Moody Press, 1999, c1980), 51-53

At the heart of the meaning of the root is the idea of
certainty. And this is borne out by the NT definition of faith
found in Heb 11:1…In the Hiphil (causative), it basically
means "to cause to be certain, sure" or "to be certain
about," "to be assured." In this sense the word in the
Hiphil conjugation is the biblical word for "to believe" and
shows that biblical faith is an assurance, a certainty, in
contrast with modem concepts of faith as something
possible, hopefully true, but not certain.[53]

Swanson takes a very similar tack, and provides some cross references

with Louw-Nida (all with πιστεύω) that are helpful:

8. LN 31.102-31.107 (hif) **believe**, put faith, trust, have
confidence, i.e., have faith as a believer in what God has
revealed (Ge 15:6; Ex 4:5; Jnh 3:5); **9.** LN 31.35-31.49
(hif) **believe to be true**, be confident of (Ge 45:26; Dt
28:66)[54]

Brown-Driver-Briggs also gives an entry for אָמַן that is helpful, though it

is perplexing as to why they would list the obscure and unique reference in

Job first and then only secondarily list the far more common and

semantically useful information:

1. *stand firm* Jb 39:24 (*c.* neg. of the horse when the
trumpet sounds Di De MV RVm; but *neither believeth* RV,
hardly trusts Da). **2.** *trust, believe:* (*a*) abs. Ex 4:31 (J) Is
7:9; 28:16 Hb 1:5 ψ 116:10 Jb 29:24; (*b*) with ל of person,

---

[53] Ibid. It is to be noted that this idea of assurance being tied to faith is similar to that of Calvin
who felt that assurance is the essence of saving faith. This concept of faith by Calvin was
rejected by the Westminster Confession, believing Calvin to be in error. Section 18.3 in the
Confession says:

This infallible assurance doth not so belong to the essence of faith, but
that a true believer may wait long, and conflict with many difficulties,
before he be partaker of it:(1) yet, being enabled by the Spirit to know the
things which are freely given him of God, he may, without extraordinary
revelation, in the right use of ordinary means, attain thereunto.(2) And
therefore it is the duty of everyone to give all diligence to make his
calling and election sure;(3) that thereby his heart may be enlarged in
peace and joy in the Holy Ghost, in love and thankfulness to God, and in
strength and cheerfulness in the duties of obedience,(4) the proper fruits
of this assurance: so far is it from inclining men to looseness.

[54]James Swanson, *Dictionary of Biblical Languages With Semantic Domains : Hebrew (Old
Testament)*, (electronic ed.; Oak Harbor: Logos Research Systems, Inc., 1997), HGK586.

trust to, believe Gn 45:26 (E) Ex 4:1, 8 (J) Je 40:14 2 Ch
32:15; with God Dt 9:23 Is 43:10; לְ of thing Ex 4:8, 9 (J) ψ
106:24 1 K 10:7 2 Ch 9:6 Is 53:1 Pr 14:15; (c) with בְּ of
person, trust in, believe in Ex 19:9 (J) 1 S 27:12 2 Ch 20:20
Jb 4:18; 15:15 Pr 26:25 Je 12:6 Mi 7:5; the usual construction
with God Gn 15:6 (E) Ex 14:31 Nu 14:11 (J) 20:12 (P) Dt
1:32 2 K 17:14 2 Ch 20:20 ψ 78:22 Jon 3:5; with בְּ of thing
Dt 28:66 Jb 15:31; 24:22; 39:12 ψ 78:32; 106:12; 119:66; (d)
with בְּ ‐ יְ trust or believe that Ex 4:5 (J) Jb 9:16 La 4:12; (e)
so with infin. Jb 15:22 ψ 27:13 (sq. לְ); also trust to do a thing,
almost = allow, Ju 11:20.

Jepsen[56] notes that the Hiphil form of אָמַן is difficult to constrain

lexically, as can be seen from the variance of translations and explanations

that have been offered. He goes on to distinguish the usage in Isaiah 7:9

(and its' interpretation in 2 Chronicles 20:20) in a manner that is consistent

with the idea of passive acceptance or trust:

> That which follows in the narrative shows what is
> meant by "believe" here. Israel does nothing at all. At
> Yahweh's inducement, the enemies destroy one another,
> and Israel merely brings home the spoil. Here, however,
> Isaiah's admonition seems to have been interpreted in a
> very unilateral manner, in the sense of doing nothing, and
> leaving everything to God alone.[57]

In final analysis, Jepsen concludes that the best paraphrases for the Hiphil

of אָמַן are "to gain stability, to rely on someone, to give credence to a

message or to consider it to be true, to trust in someone."[58]

Another analysis of the Hiphil of אָמַן is made by Walter Moberly.[59]

Moberly points to Genesis 15:6 as a controlling indicator of the semantic

meaning of אָמַן, noting that it occurs with a *waw* consecutive in the Hiphil

---

[55]Francis Brown et al., *Enhanced Brown-Driver-Briggs Hebrew and English Lexicon*, electronic
ed. (Oak Harbor, WA: Logos Research Systems, 2000), s.v. אָמַן

[56] "אָמַן" in *TDOT*, 298

[57] Ibid, 306-307

[58] Ibid, 308

[59] "אָמַן" in William A. VanGemeren, ed. *The New international Dictionary of Old Testament
Theology and Exegesis, Vol. 1* (Grand Rapids, MI; Zondervan, 1997).

perfect.[60] Moberly notes that this indicates that Abraham's faith was
continuous and obedient; however, he never considers in his analysis that the
LXX translators decided that the best translation of וְהֶאֱמִן was the aorist
ἐπίστευσεν rather than an imperfect, which would have conveyed the intent
that Moberly infers. The LXX translators simply did not see the continuing
aspect that Moberly does. Contextually it seems his analysis is doubtful in
this instance. Near the end of his entry we find:

> One of the points that is unclear is how this faith is to
> be displayed. Does it mean trusting God and "keeping the
> powder dry" (i.e. taking appropriate military action), or
> does it mean trusting God and taking no action? Generally
> speaking, the normal OT (and biblical) pattern is the
> former- trust in God is the context, not a substitute, for
> appropriate action. However, there are exceptional
> circumstances where the emphasis is entirely on trusting
> God and letting him do everything that needs to be done;
> Israel's deliverance from Egypt at the Red Sea (Exod 14)
> is a classic example.[61]

His evidence seems to cast doubt on his earlier conclusions regarding the
meaning of the word. This work is a theological dictionary and not a
lexicon, so some interpretation and expansion is to be expected. However,
the exception(s) to the rule of continuation in or necessary action from אָמַן
show that these things can only be inferred contextually and therefore are
not, by definition, a part of the semantic range of the word.

By looking at the lexical entries it becomes readily apparent that in the
Hiphil stem the verb אָמַן carries the simple denotation of "to believe" or to
"trust." However, that does not completely solve the problem, as there are

---

[60] Ibid, 432

[61] Ibid. The nuance of obedience as an intrinsic and essential aspect of faith has been made into
a theological dictum by Dan Fuller in *The Unity of the Bible: Unfolding God's Plan for
Humanity* (Grand Rapids, MI; Zondervan, 1992) and John Piper, *Future Grace* (Sisters, OR;
Multnomah Publishers, 1995). For an analysis of this theological perspective see Fred Chay,
Neo-Legalism.

some scholars who follow the work of Bultmann[62] and carry the idea of perseverance and continued faithfulness into the meaning of the word. It seems, though, that by looking at several uses in context that only contextual clues, and not semantics and lexical considerations, can in certain instances lead to the conclusion that a given instance of אָמַן in the Hiphil (and hence the LXX translation of πιστεύω) carry endurance. It seems that the word itself does not have that denotation inherent within it.

Some scholars point to 2 Kings 12:15 to establish a perseverance aspect to faith terminology in the Septuagint. The text reads, "Moreover, they did not require an accounting from the men into whose hand they gave the money to pay to those who did the work, for they dealt faithfully (πίστις/אֱמֻנָה)." The same logic is applied to texts such as Hosea 2:20, "And I will betroth you to Me in faithfulness (πίστις/אֱמוּנָה). Then you will know the Lord." The major error in such a judgment is importing verbal ideas into nouns. In both of these instances nouns have been translated, and by definition nouns have no aspectual force. Importing verbal force into cognate nouns is treacherous at best, and if there can be demonstrated instances of the verb where perseverance is either not required or plainly illogical, then importing the idea of noun uses into the verb is best avoided.

An instance of this very thing is readily at hand in the use of the verb in the Exodus. Consider the following texts from the account of Exodus 4 and 14:

> "So the people believed (aorist indicative of πιστεύω);
> and when they heard that the Lord was concerned about
> the sons of Israel and that He had seen their affliction, then
> they bowed low and worshiped." Exodus 4:31

> "When Israel saw the great power which the Lord had used
> against the Egyptians, the people feared the Lord, and they

---

[62] See, for example, Kenneth Gentry, "The Great Option: A Study of the Lordship Controversy," *Baptist Reformation Review* 5 (1976), 49-79

believed (aorist indicative of πιστεύω) in the Lord and in
His servant Moses." Exodus 14:31

However else we view the eternal state of these people, there can be no
doubt as to what the text says: the people exercised πιστεύω in Yahweh
(clearly in 14:31). This belief manifested itself in the song of commitment to
Yahweh in 15:1-21. Yet three short days later, at 15:24, the song of praise
and commitment had been turned to grumbling and complaining (see also
16:4, 24). Looking further, when we compare their attitude in Numbers
14:11, it can help to ascertain the semantic range of the word in the LXX:

"The Lord said to Moses, "How long will this people
spurn Me? And how long will they not believe (present
indicative of πιστεύω) in Me, despite all the signs which I
have performed in their midst?"

The same people who exercised πιστεύω in Exodus 4 had certainly made
a change by the time of Numbers 14. As a result all but two of them (Joshua
and Caleb) died in the wilderness as a result of their unbelief. Consideration
must also be given to texts such as Numbers 20:12:

But the Lord said to Moses and Aaron, "Because you have
not believed (aorist indicative of πιστεύω) Me, to treat Me
as holy in the sight of the sons of Israel, therefore you shall
not bring this assembly into the land which I have given
them."

Even Moses and Aaron did not continue in their belief. The Lord
chastised them severely for their failure to continue in belief, and it cost
them entrance into the land of Canaan[63]. Aaron and Moses, two men who

---

[63] If entrance into the land of Canaan is a type of entering heaven in the NT, as some have
claimed, then only two of the potentially millions of Hebrews who left Egypt had exercised
salvific faith. This seems untenable, not only on the basis of the fact that they had to paint the
doorposts and lintels with blood (a clear allusion to trust in Yahweh) to save their firstborn son,
and even more so when we consider that Moses never made it to Canaan. If ever there was a
hero of the faith it was Moses, who according to Hebrews 11:24-30 is a hero of the faith, and

had continually seen Yahweh and been His mouthpieces, failed to continue

in that faith at the point of the Lord's wrath in Num 20:12. Πιστεύω in the

LXX, then, can be shown to fail to persevere, which indicates that ongoing

obedience may not be imported into the semantic range of the word.

Another important aspect of any Hebrew word study is a treatment of

related or parallel/near-synonymous terms. When studying πιστεύω in the

LXX and its' Hebrew root אָמַן, the student does indeed find an additional

term that is helpful in understanding the semantic range. Psalm 78:22 (77:22

LXX) provides, by way of expansion and restatement, some help in

understanding πιστεύω in the LXX:

Because they did not believe in God and did not trust in His salvation.

ὅτι οὐκ ἐπίστευσαν ἐν τῷ θεῷ οὐδὲ ἤλπισαν ἐπὶ τὸ σωτήριον

αὐτοῦ.[64]

כִּי לֹא הֶאֱמִינוּ בֵּאלֹהִים וְלֹא בָטְחוּ בִּישׁוּעָתוֹ:[65]

Here we see the combination of אָמַן/πιστεύω and also the combination of

בָּטַח/ἐλπίζω. The same occurrence of both words occurs in Micah 7:5 and

these two instances provide the exegete an opportunity to further assess the

semantic range of πιστεύω in the LXX. A study of בָּטַח will assist us in

according to Matthew 17:3; Mark 9:4, and Luke 9:30 appeared with Elijah at the transfiguration
and clearly and unambiguously was regenerate. Entrance into Canaan cannot be made a type of
entrance to heaven if there are exceptions to the rule (even for someone as great as Moses),
because there are absolutely no exceptions for the requirement for entrance into heaven
according to John 14:6.
The O.T. theology of forgiveness is rendered problematic in this view since Moses pleaded for
the forgiveness of sin for these people and God gave it. In Numbers 14:20-22 how could it be
that God would forgive them for their sin of rebellion and then not allow them to enter the land
if the entrance to the land is to be seen as a type of heaven? This would mean that they went to
eternal damnation if this theology is utilized in the Book of Hebrews 3-4 as a type. The logical
consequences of this view render it problematic at best, and best avoided.
[64]*Septuaginta : With morphology*, (Stuttgart: Deutsche Bibelgesellschaft, 1996, c1979), Ps
77:22.
[65]*Biblia Hebraica Stuttgartensia : With Westminster Hebrew Morphology.*, (electronic ed.;
Stuttgart; Glenside PA: German Bible Society; Westminster Seminary, 1996, c1925;
morphology c1991), Ps 78:22.

analyzing the semantic range of πιστεύω in the LXX. A list of every occurrence of the verb אָמַן in the LXX is found in Appendix 4.

The study on בָּטַח in NIDOTTE is also done by Moberly, and this helps us by establishing some continuity in interpretive framework (even in light of Moberly's analysis of Genesis 15:6). The glosses provided by NIDOTTE are "trust, hiph. put one's trust in; be full of confidence, feel safe."[66] Moberly goes on to provide this helpful explanation:

> The range of meaning of bṭḥ and mibṭāḥ in Heb. is similar to that of "trust" in Eng. That is, trust can be placed in a large number of different people or things and can often be misplaced. God is the supreme object of trust, and some of the things in which people put their trust are substitutes for God, however naturally worthy of trust they may appear to be in themselves. Thus, people can often put their trust in riches (Job 31:24; Ps. 49:6[7]; 62:10[11]; Prov 11:28), in powerful people (Ps. 146:3), in strongly fortified cities (Deut 28:52; Jer 5:17), or in their own cleverness (Prov 3:5; 28:26)-all in contexts where the writer views these as negative things, alternatives to trusting in God.[67]

TDOT has this additional insight on בָּטַח:

> ...frequently bṭḥ is used to describe a person who thinks he is secure, but is deceived because the object on which his feeling of security is based is unreliable. When we take all the passages in which bṭḥ is used in this sense, we get a picture of everything to which the heart of man clings and on which he believes he can build his life, but which will end in failure.[68]

Jepsen goes on to state,

> "The community of Yahweh can know for sure that it can rely on him...these passages are held together by a common bond, viz., that in time of need, whatever it may

---

[66] R. W. L. Moberly, "בָּטַח" in *NIDOTTE*, 644
[67] Ibid, 645
[68] Alfred Jepsen, בָּטַח in TDOT, Vol 1, 90

be, there is no way for man to survive but to take refuge in
Yahweh, to trust in him, and to have confidence in him."[69]

This word, then, appears to contain the idea commonly referred to in
modern theological ideology as *fiducia*, the clinging, ongoing trust that
commits itself to the object of the trust. Here we find the Reformed concept
of commitment and submission to the Lordship of Yahweh. Given this, it is
most interesting to note the manner in which the translators of the LXX
chose to translate בָּטַח. There are 117 occurrences in BHS of the verb בָּטַח,
and of these 58 are rendered by the Greek πείθω. These occurrences are
especially clustered in Proverbs, Isaiah, and Jeremiah. The above discussion
on πείθω bears weight here as well. An additional 57 occurrences are
translated as ἐλπίζω or one of its compounds, or as its noun cognate ἐλπίς
in the translation of a few substantival participles. These occurrences are
especially concentrated in the Psalms[70].

It must certainly not escape the exegete that this word, which seems to
encompass the ongoing trust and commitment of *fiducia* so sought after in
faith, is *never once* translated by the word πιστεύω. The translators of the
LXX evidently saw something in בָּטַח that caused them to completely avoid
πιστεύω in translation. Instead, they felt that "hope" or "convince/set at
ease" best rendered the intent of the author.

In that the translators chose a specific word to translate into πιστεύω, and
that they used completely different words when translating similar terms, it
would be unwise to blur the distinction they so carefully and seemingly
deliberately set up. Though we might be tempted to synonymize these

---

[69] Ibid, 92-93

[70] In the Psalms, the LXX uses ἐλπίζω 38 times, versus only 5 uses of πείθω. A thorough study
of usage in the Psalms is beyond the scope of this paper, though it is generally observed that the
Psalms are the strongest references to the abiding trust and commitment to Yahweh in the face
of danger and opposition. The predominant use of ἐλπίζω, "hope" with its connotation of a
futuristic focus and continuing emphasis, fits this focus nicely.

words by tracing πιστεύω through its root πιθ to πείθω and declaring them synonymous, we must resist in light of the LXX translators resistance to the same temptation. To do so would commit both the root fallacy *and* Barr's illegitimate identity transfer at the same time, taking the semantic range of one word and transferring it to another that does not share its semantic range *in toto*.

It would seem that πιστεύω in the LXX cannot be demonstrated to mandate continuing belief or obedience; instances such as this (as well as the life of Abraham, David, and Solomon to name but a few) require the semantic value of the word to stay constrained to simple trust or confidence, with no durative force inherent in the term. As a rule, we must also heed the warning of Barth:

> How πιστεύειν and πίστις became *the* central
> theological terms for the appropriate relationship to God
> and for the Christian religion itself cannot be clarified from
> the perspective of this Jewish background alone. Here one
> must take account of a further, independent Christian
> development prompted by events themselves.[71]

The Septuagint can help us see the development of the term, and can provide some insight into the study of faith terminology of the New Testament. However, as Barth has wisely cautioned, only a study of the terminology in context in the New Testament can provide a definitive answer.

---

[71] G. Barth, "πίστις/ πιστεύειν, #4190" in Horst Balz and Gerhard Schneider, eds., *The Exegetical Dictionary of the New Testament* (Grand Rapids, MI; Eerdmans, 1991), 3:91

Syntactical Issues:

Having completed our word study and lexical analysis of πιστεύω, we must now turn our attention to grammatical and syntactical considerations. Words only acquire meaning as they are used in context,[72] and so our attention naturally turns next to specific occurrences and patterns of usage with πιστεύω that can be found in the New Testament. By analyzing the syntactical considerations surrounding πιστεύω we can further refine our understanding of the faith that saves.

There is wide agreement among evangelical scholars that to "believe into" the name of Christ is a statement of saving faith. This combination (πιστεύω + εἰς) is common in the Greek New Testament, and occurs over thirty times in the Gospel of John alone. This seems fitting for the gospel account which gives the fullest and clearest view of the doctrine of eternal life. It appears that the usage of this construction refers to genuine, saving faith.[73] The following chart gives every instance of this construction in the New Testament:

πιστεύω εἰς	
Salvific	Non – salvific
Matthew 18:6 Mark 9:42 John 1:12 John 2:11, 23 John 3:16, 18, 36 John 4:39 John 6:29, 35, 40 John 7:5, 31, 38, 39, 48 John 8:30	None, unless John 12:42 is a sole exception to the pattern.

---

[72] We are reminded here of the maxim that "a text, without its' context, is merely a pretext."

[73] It is readily acknowledged that some scholars dispute the nature of belief in John 12:42. This usage is discussed in detail below. This one instance notwithstanding, every other instance (whether in John's writings or in another authors' usage) is indicative of salvific faith. The very fact that John uses the phrase 30 times to refer to genuine conversions should give the exegete pause when disputing the nature of the faith mentioned in John 12:42.

John 9:35, 36 John 10:42 John 11:25, 26, 45, 48 John 12:36, 37, 42, 44, 46 John 14:1, 12 John 16:9 Acts 10:43 Romans 4:8 Romans 10:10 I John 5:10, 13	

There is general scholarly agreement that this syntactical combination is indicative of genuine belief. The problem arises when the claim is made that most of the time this combination is the *only* use that refers to saving faith. This would mean that to believe *in* (πιστεύω ἐν), believe *that* (πιστεύω ὅτι), or believe *upon* (πιστεύω ἐπὶ) would not constitute saving faith in normative New Testament usage. Botha elaborates on this misconception:

> "What is also significant is the typical misconception that a certain construction in Greek bears a certain meaning. The fact that pisteuo eis is used often in John is meaningful only in that it reflects his personal style and preference. There is no real difference between pisteuo eis and other constructions wherein pisteuo can also occur – it is only convention of the language and nothing more."[74]

The thought that only πιστεύω εἰς refers to genuine, eschatologically salvific faith is extremely unfortunate for those who lean on John 3 as a key passage for studying the doctrine of soteriology! John 3:16 is used widely to show the path to eternal deliverance from damnation (and rightly so), but in verse 15 John uses the terminology πιστεύω ἐν with seemingly clear salvific value, so if true saving belief is not meant there then 3:16 loses

---

[74] J.E. Botha, "Pisteuo in the Greek New Testament", 229 See Kenneth Gentry, "The Great Option" for the genesis of the syntactical issue. A similar line of thought is seen in Walter Chantry's *Today's Gospel: Authentic or Synthetic?* (Carlisle, PA; Banner of Truth Trust; 1970). A more recent proponent of this line of thinking built off syntactical grounds is Norman Geisler *Systematic Theology Vol 3* (Minneapolis, MN; Bethany House 2004), 323, 519.

soteriological value as well. In order to get a better grasp on this dilemma, consider the following charts:

πιστεύω ἐν	
Salvific	Non – salvific
Mark 1:15	I Thessalonians 1:7
John 3:15	
Romans 10:9	
I Timothy 3:16	

V πιστεύω ὅτι	
Salvific	Non – salvific
John 8:24	Matthew 9:28
John 11:27	Mark 11:23, 24
John 16:27, 30 (possible)	Luke 1:45
John 17:8, 21 (possible)	John 11:42
John 20:31	John 14:10
I Thessalonians 4:14	Acts 9:26
I John 5:1, 5	Romans 6:8
	James 2:19

V πιστεύω ἐπὶ	
Salvific	Non – salvific
Matthew 27:42	Luke 24:25 (possible)
Acts 11:17	
Acts 16:31	
Acts 22:19	
Romans 4:24	
Romans 9:33	
Romans 10:11	
I Timothy 1:16	
I Peter 2:6	

Take note that with regard to the use of πιστεύω with ἐν and ἐπὶ, only one verse in each chart seems to be non-salvific. With ὅτι the sides are fairly evenly balanced, although notice that all but one of the salvific uses occur in John's writings. This is somewhat significant considering the salvific nature of his entire gospel account. Also it seems that πιστεύω εἰς and πιστεύω ἐν convey the same basic meaning.[75] This makes sense of the fact that John uses both constructions in John 3 to get across Jesus' idea of belief that leads to eternal life.[76]

Syntactically, then, it is clear that the exegete must carefully determine whether any given New Testament use of πιστεύω indicates salvific belief rather than pursuing blanket categories.[77] This analysis must spring from

---

[75] Daniel Wallace, in *Greek Grammar Beyond the Basics*, (Grand Rapids, MI; Zondervan, 1996), 359, explains:

> πιστεύω + ἐν is the equivalent of πιστεύω + εἰς (cf. Mark 1:15; John 3:15). The idea is "put one's faith *into*" even though ἐν is used. What is the value of this discussion for exegesis? It is simply that too often prepositions are analyzed simplistically, etymologically, and without due consideration for the verb to which they are connected. Prepositions are often treated in isolation, as though their ontological meaning were still completely intact.

Wallace also lists in the uses of both prepositions that in Koine they can be used in place of one another (369, 372), though he states on 372 that ἐν is only an equivalent for εἰς for verbs of motion.

[76] The charts above show the usages. Πιστεύω + ἐν is the first occurrence in 3:15; Πιστεύω + εἰς is then used in verses 16, 18, and 36.

[77] For those who hold that there is a distinction between πιστεύω εἰς and πιστεύω ὅτι, the words of Schnackenburg are insightful in his commentary on John. He concludes, "In many texts πιστεύω εἰς is on the same footing as a ὅτι clause . . . and often the absolute πιστεύειν means the Johannine faith in the fullest sense. . . ." (John Schnackenburg, *The Gospel According to John*, 1:561).

For those seeking the distinction of πιστεύω εἰς, a simple look at a variety of passages that are clearly salvific are helpful in the Gospel of John (1:12; 2:11; 2:23; 3:16; 3:18a, 18c, 4:39; 6:29; 6:35; 6:40; 7:5. For πιστεύω with a dative, consult John 2:22; 4:21; 4:50; 5:24; 5:38; 5:46; 5:47; 6:38; 6:31; 8:45; 8:46. For πιστεύω ὅτι, John 4:21; 6:69; 8:24; 11:27; 11:42; 13:19; 14:10; 16:27; 16:30; 17:8). By way of example, a construction with a ὅτι clause which is clearly salvific is found in John 8:24, "...believe that I am He..." John 20:31 provides an additional example, "...believe that Jesus is the Christ...."

Richard Christianson, in his thesis, "The Soteriological Significance of Πιστεύω in the Gospel of John", says this:

> The difference between the πιστεύω εἰς and πιστεύω ὅτι constructions is not one of meaning. Both mean one and the same thing: voluntary acceptance of a specific proposition. The difference between the two constructions is that πιστεύω ὅτι introduces an explicit statement of the proposition which is accepted while πιστεύω εἰς does not. The πιστεύω εἰς construction thus functions as an abbreviation for the πιστεύω ὅτι construction (86-87).

Leon Morris, no friend of "Free Grace", also makes a similar conclusion in his book *The Gospel According to John* in *The New International Commentary on the New Testament* (Grand Rapids, MI; Eerdmans, 1995):

> The conclusion to which we come is that, while each of the various

semantic range but more importantly from context and other indicators. It would seem that a renewed focus upon the hermeneutical principle of observation and assessment of context will assist the exegete in a much greater way than allegiance to any particular theological doctrine.

---

constructions employed has its own proper sense; they must not be too sharply separated from one another. Basic is the idea of that activity of believing which takes the believer out of himself and makes him one with Christ. But really to believe the Father or really to believe the facts about Christ inevitably involves this activity. Whichever way the terminology is employed it stresses the attitude of trustful reliance on God, which is basic for the Christian (337).

Grammatical Issues:

One of the weightiest issues in the debate over the nature of faith is that of verbal aspect and time force. Greek verbs are defined under three categories; tense, voice, and mood. It is important for this discussion to understand how these categories work together, especially tense and mood. It is generally agreed that there are two functional elements to verb tense, namely aspect (portrayal of action with respect to progress, results, or simple occurrence[78]) and time (when the action occurred). Wallace clarifies the order of importance: "Aspect is the primary value of tense in Greek and time is secondary, if involved at all."[79] In other words what is mainly under consideration is how the action is portrayed as occurring.

Lordship proponents argue that when πιστεύω is used it normally means that the nature of belief is continuous. Normally this argument is made when πιστεύω occurs in the present tense. Frequently time and aspect are confused, and we get a statement such as this: "John Doe is presently believing and it is implied he will continue in this state."

It is worth remembering at this point that time is almost non-existent outside the confines of the indicative mood. In other words, a verb is not always described as occurring at the present time simply because it is in the present tense. It could be past time or future time (depending upon context), and outside the indicative there is no independent statement as to where a given verb falls time-wise. As Appendix 1 illustrates, πιστεύω occurs frequently outside the indicative mood.

Another interesting thing to note in this discussion is that belief is often shown in the aorist tense. The aorist tense normally denotes a statement of simple occurrence with no respect to duration. In the indicative it normally indicates past time. The name aorist "was given to this tense by

---

[78] Daniel Wallace, *Greek Grammar*, 499
[79] Ibid, 496

grammarians to denote that the action spoken of is to be regarded simply as an event, without any regard to the time in which it occurs or the length of time during which it has been going on."[80] Πιστεύω occurs in the aorist tense over 20 times in the book of John alone, with at least three of these in the subjunctive mood (i.e., outside the indicative mood). This is fairly significant, especially when John uses the aorist subjunctive in John 1:7 when stating what the goal of Jesus' ministry would be. It would appear that John is not concerned so much with whether a person continues believing, as much as whether or not belief has occurred.

Exegesis must utilize grammar, but it is not the end of the story, nor can it solve every exegetical issue within the text. It is also important to understand that grammar must be used correctly and not ambiguously to make a theological point. This includes the often repeated dictum that the present tense means continual action and therefore when "faith" terminology occurs in the text it means "continue to believe" or "continual faith." Exegetes should have learned their lesson from the issue of the "abused aorist" brought to the forefront by Frank Stagg years ago.[81] His grammatical analysis corrected an error of exegesis in the overuse or misapplication of the fallacious "once for all" action that was supposedly bound up in the aorist tense. His work has been a watershed for biblical scholarship. Unfortunately, modern exegetes seem to have forgotten the lesson that Stagg brought, or at least have failed to grasp the significance of his analysis for tenses other than the aorist.

It is often common to hear that the present tense means continual action or durative-linear action.[82] There is a large degree of truth to this maxim of grammar, in that the *default* aspect of the present tense is durative or

---

[80] David A. Black *It's Still Greek to Me.* (Grand Rapids, MI; Baker Book House, 1998), 104.

[81] Frank Stagg, "The Abused Aorist," *Journal of Biblical Literature* 91 (1972), 222-31.

[82] See the standard grammars for NT Greek: H. E. Dana and Julius R. Mantey, *A Manual of the Greek New Testament* (Toronto: The Macmillian Company, 1957), 182; C. F. D. Moule, *An Idiom Book of New Testament Greek* (Cambridge: Cambridge University Press, 1959), 7; A. T. Robertson, *Grammar of the Greek New Testament: in Light of Historical Research* (Nashville, TN; Broadman & Holman Publishers, 1947), 879.

imperfective. The unfortunate result in some exegesis is that when one sees the present tense it causes a reflex reaction that concludes that it must mean, or normally means, that for the action to be actual or genuine it must be continual because of the "meaning of the present tense."

This misuse of grammar leads to the theological interpretation that states that when a person truly believes the gospel, the faith that is biblical or saving is the faith that continues. Hence if a person's faith does not continue it is, by the assumed definition of the tense, non-saving faith or spurious faith (to use Calvin's category). Therefore it is relegated to "demon faith" or a "Judas faith," but not saving faith because of the lack of continuance. It is argued that in the New Testament genuine faith is seen most often in present tense. Dan Wallace, my (Fred's) former teacher, put it this way in his class on intermediate grammar: "John's tendency is to use a progressive or completed tense (either imperfect, present, or perfect) for a belief which leads to salvation (e.g. in 3:16 he uses the present participle) but an undefined or punctiliar tense (aorist) for belief which stops short of true salvation."

The exegete and theologian must ask the questions, "Is this always true? Is it normative? Is it even valid?" Dr. Wallace's *magnum opus* is his excellent book, *Greek Grammar Beyond the Basics*, but he has also completed a recent and shorter version, *Basics of New Testament Syntax*. Wallace correctly tells the reader in his shorter grammar, *BNTS*:

> ... in Matt[hew] 5:28, "everyone who looks at a woman" (πᾶς ὁ βλέπων γυναῖκα) with lust in his heart does not mean "continually looking" or "habitually looking," any more than four verses later [5:32] "everyone who divorces his wife" (πᾶς ὁ ἀπολύων τὴν γυναῖκα αὐτοῦ) means "repeatedly divorces"![83]

---

[83] Daniel B. Wallace, *The Basics of New Testament Syntax* (Grand Rapids, MI; Zondervan, 2000), 268; Wallace, *Greek Grammar,*, 616.

For those who assume that present participles prove or mandate continuing action, the problem of such a conclusion can be seen in Mark 6:14. Herod calls John "the baptizing one," using a present attributive participle ὁ βαπτίζων. However, Herod clearly did not mean that John continued baptizing during his imprisonment or after his death.[84] The use of the present tense would allow for calling David "the murdering one" (e.g., "the murderer"). However no one would interpret it to mean the David is still murdering people centuries after dying. In fact, it does not even imply that he murdered anyone besides Uriah. The attributive present participle as a point of grammar says nothing about either the continuation or the repetition of the action. This fallacy is similar to that made concerning the abused aorist meaning a once for all action. In Wallace's shorter work he clearly defines this important point of grammar.

In his larger grammar, though, he seems to reverse himself after his repeated warnings about over-interpreting present participles.[85] In this work he makes a theological conclusion based on a point of grammar:

> The aspectual force of the present ὁ πιστεύων seems to be in contrast with ὁ πιστεύσας. The aorist is used only eight times (plus two in the longer ending of Mark). The aorist is sometimes used to describe believers as such and thus has a generic force (cf. for the clearest example the *v.l.* at Mark 16:16; cf. also 2 Thess 1:10; Heb 4:3; perhaps John 7:39; also, negatively, of those who did not [μή] believe: 2 Thess 2:12; Jude 5). The present occurs six times as often (43 times), most often in soteriological contexts (cf. John 1:12; 3:15, 16, 18; 3:36; 6:35, 47, 64; 7:38; 11:25; 12:46; Acts 2:44; 10:43; 13:39; Rom 1:16; 3:22; 4:11, 24; 9:33; 10:4, 11; 1 Cor 1:21; 14:22 [*bis*]; Gal 3:22; Eph 1:19; 1 Thess 1:7; 2:10, 13; 1 Pet 2:6, 7; 1 John 5:1, 5, 10, 13). Thus, it seems that since the aorist participle was a live option to describe a "believer," it is unlikely that when the present was used, it was aspectually flat. The present was the tense of choice most likely because the NT writers by

---

[84] Wallace, in *Greek Grammar*, 620, agrees regarding Mark 6:14, but in *Basics of Syntax*, he does not mention it.
[85] Daniel Wallace, *Greek Grammar*, 616 and 620-621; cf. *Basics of Syntax*, 268.

and large saw *continual* belief as a necessary condition of salvation. Along these lines, it seems significant that the *promise* of salvation is almost always given to ὁ πιστεύων (cf. several of the above-cited texts), almost never to ὁ πιστεύσας (apart from Mark 16:16, John 7:39 and Heb 4:3 come the closest [the present tense of πιστεύω never occurs in Hebrews]). [86]

We must analyze the specifics of these statements to see if they can withstand close scrutiny:

1. The tense and the use of the participle favor continual action. Therefore faith must be continual to be genuine. He states:

   > John 3:16 πᾶς ὁ πιστεύων everyone who believes[.] The idea seems to be both gnomic and continual: "everyone who continually believes." This is not due to the present tense only, but to the use of the present participle of πιστεύω, especially in soteriological contexts in the NT. [87]

   How does he validate or verify this point? Wallace considers the tense used in the substantival participle with the use of πιστεύω. Present substantival uses occur about six times as often as aorists. It must be noted here that Wallace seems to violate the principle of single meaning in describing the use of the present participle in John 3:16 as "both gnomic and continual." As Botha pointed out above in our lexical inquiry[88], the participle here *cannot* be both gnomic and continual. It must be either one or the other; by trying to make it mean both, Wallace has committed the illegitimate totality transfer.

2. A theological doctrine is established:

---

[86] Wallace, *Greek Grammar*, 621, n. 22.
[87] Daniel Wallace, *Basics of Syntax*, 271; and *Greek Grammar*, 621.
[88] See J.E. Botha, "Pisteuo in the Greek New Testament", 233-34.

> The present was the tense of choice most likely
> because the NT writers by and large saw
> *continual* belief as a necessary condition of
> salvation.[89]

Notice the wiggle room, "by and large." He must use this concession since this argumentation seems to invalidate itself in light of the fact that John uses the aorist in 4:39, 41, and 17:8 in referring to genuine salvation. If John saw continual belief as necessary we would not expect to find instances in his writing that do not necessitate this.

3. Therefore, he restates. He admits that the aorist "is sometimes used to describe believers as such and thus has a generic force."[90] The point, though, is that the normal use of the present tense is to indicate that faith is to be continual (and that the aorist is not fitting for this purpose). Is this proof? We can look at his reasoning that reduces to three points based on the formal use of the present tense and statistical function:

    a. Both aorist and present participles depict believers,
    b. Present participles are more common (statistically) for πιστεύω,
    c. Therefore, believing is necessarily continuous action.

The form of the syllogism is right (2 premises and a conclusion), but notice an analogy to its contents and the error it creates:

> The Greek New Testament uses the articular
> present participle more often (Matthew 5:32 and
> Luke 16:18) than the articular aorist participle
> (Mark 10:12) to describe divorce.[91] Thus,
> Matthew 5:32 and Luke 16:18 would refer to one

---

[89] Ibid.
[90] Ibid.
[91] See Daniel Wallace's discussion of Matthew 5:32.

who keeps on and keeps on and keeps on divorcing the same wife.[92]

The three points resemble Wallace's case for πιστεύω:

a.   Both aorist and present participles depict divorcers,

b.   Present participles are more common for ἀπολύω,

c.   Therefore, divorcing is necessarily continuous action[?!].[93]

Wallace rightly rejects such a construct of present versus aorist substantival participles regarding divorce. He should be consistent. He should not state that a present participle does not prove continuous action, and then turn around and refute his own claim that it does, "especially in soteriological contexts in the NT." This is a classic case of special pleading.

Wallace does note in his grammar, "In particular when a participle is *substantival*, its aspectual force is more susceptible to reduction in force"[94] (italics original). He then goes on to say,

> "[M]any substantival participles in the NT are used in generic utterances. The πας ὁ ἀκουων (or ἀγαπων, ποιων, etc.) formula is always or almost always generic. As such it is expected to involve a *gnomic* idea. Most of these instances involve the present participle. But if they are already gnomic, we would be hard pressed to make something more out of them-such as a progressive idea."[95] (italics original)

However, Wallace ignores his own grammatical advice when it comes to πιστεύω. He states, concerning the phrase πᾶς ὁ πιστεύων above, "...it

---

[92] I am indebted to John Niemelä, "Book Review of The Basics of New Testament Syntax: An Intermediate Greek Grammar: The Abridgement of 'Greek Grammar Beyond the Basics,'" *CTSJ* 6:3 (July 2000): 74.

[93] Ibid.

[94] Daniel Wallace, *Grammar*, 615

[95] Ibid, 615-616

seems that since the aorist participle was a live option to describe a 'believer,' it is unlikely that when the present was used, it was aspectually flat."[96] Thus he breaks his own admonition. He does so without any serious analysis of why he would break his rule of grammar, other than the fact that the aorist was a "live option."

In the first place, we must exegete according to what the author wrote, not what he could have written. In the second place, Wallace's logic is a case of special pleading based on the presence of πιστεύω. It is unwise in the extreme to make special exceptions for words just because they are theologically important, especially when we would do so on theological rather than textual grounds (such as John's supposed emphasis on continual belief). Wallace would not make a case that the aorist participle was a live option for "those who hear" or "those who love" above and therefore the present participle πας ὁ ἀκουων carries a durative concept. Thus consistency demands he not demand it for πᾶς ὁ πιστεύων either.

The danger of placing too fine a point on grammar to make a dogmatic and absolute theological pronouncement can be seen above. It is one of the dangers that an exegete must be aware of, lest their theology direct their exegesis and turn it into eisegesis. Wallace has read a continual belief into John 3:16 where his own grammar denies that use. He needs to be consistent in his analysis and his exegesis. Continual belief is no more in mind in John 3:16 than continual baptizing is in view in Mark 6:14.

With this in mind, it becomes clear that it is dangerous indeed to assume that the normative use of the word πιστεύω is always continuous action, especially in light of the fact that it cannot even be assumed that the present tense in general assumes continuous aspect. While many theologians discuss "aspect" in a verb, in reality they are discussing its' *Aktionsart*, which combines aspect with lexical, grammatical, and contextual features to

---

[96] Ibid, 621 footnote 22

interpret the verb. As Wallace points out, *Aktionsart* is neither objective nor simplistic to determine.[97]

Another point that should be made clear is that while participles can have time and aspect, they are inextricably dependent on the main verb. A great many uses of πιστεύω are participles, and while participles basically translate with a sense of action in time (often present time), the main verb controls the timing of the action of a participle. Many theological arguments are based on a misunderstanding of participles.

Grammatically, then, the argument for continual belief is weak. We have seen that syntactically we cannot constrict salvific belief to a given construction. We have further seen that grammatical considerations militate against finding continual belief in instances such as substantival participles in John 3:16.

---

[97] Ibid, 499

Scripture Commentary:

After assessing the lexical and grammatical considerations, the question remains, "How should one treat the various Scripture passages which touch on this issue?" At the end of the day we must hold to the tenet of *Sola Scriptura* and look to the text itself in determining our view of faith. Therefore we must examine the controversial passages in Scripture which use πιστεύω and πίστις. It is only by a careful analysis of the Scriptures in question that we can arrive at valid conclusions.

Those who hold to Lordship salvation argue repeatedly that there are two kinds of faith in the New Testament: saving faith and non-saving faith. Does the New Testament validate that *a priori* assumption? Because Simon Magus in Acts 8 has been historically seen as someone who had a false faith and was thus unregenerate, the passage in Acts that discusses his case is an excellent place to begin our analysis of the texts that discuss the nature of faith in the New Testament.

Acts 8:9-24

This passage has engendered great debate over the eternal destiny of Simon Magus. The passage in question begins with Simon, a sorcerer, having a large following because of his magic and claims of greatness (verses 9-11). When Phillip came and preached the good news, many men and women believed and were baptized, including Simon (v. 12-13). When the Apostles hear of the opening of Samaria to the gospel, they send Peter and John to give apostolic sanction to the awakening (thus the delay in the reception of the Holy Spirit; v. 14-17). Simon sees this tremendous power wielded by the Apostles, and offers to pay them to give it to him as well (v. 18-19). This earns him a stinging rebuke from Peter (v. 20-24).

Some interpreters hold that Simon never truly believed, but only pretended for selfish gain.[98] To evaluate this position, we must take careful note of the text of 8:13:

"ὁ δὲ Σίμων καὶ αὐτὸς **ἐπίστευσεν** καὶ βαπτισθεὶς ἦν προσκαρτερῶν τῷ Φιλίππῳ, θεωρῶν τε σημεῖα καὶ δυνάμεις μεγάλας γινομένας ἐξίστατο." (Acts 8:13)

Πιστεύω occurs here in relation to Simon in the aorist active indicative. Grammatically it is not debated that Luke is presenting an event that occurred at a point in time in the past. This is a very common feature of narrative literature, to use the aorist to describe punctiliar events and the imperfect to describe ongoing or repetitive events. So the simple and clear statement of the text is that Simon believed and is included with the rest of his Samaritan contemporaries from verse 12.

Luke then comments that after Simon was baptized he continued constantly with Philip (using the imperfect periphrastic ἦν προσκαρτερῶν, "he was constantly attending to"). It seems Luke's clear intent was to convey that after his belief and baptism that Simon became a disciple of Phillip. When the Samaritans receive the Holy Spirit, it seems reasonable to assume that Simon did as well.[99]

The remainder of the passage is the source of the controversy surrounding Simon's faith. Simon became greedy and selfish and was rebuked by Peter. Peter says in verse 21 that Simon's heart "is not right before God," and in verse 23 Peter tells Simon "you are... in the bond of iniquity." The

---

[98] See Merrill Frederick Unger, "The Baptism with the Holy Spirit" in *Bibliotheca Sacra 101:404* (October 1944), 483; see also R. Bruce Compton "Persevering and Falling Away: A Reexamination of Hebrews 6:4-6" in *Detroit Baptist Seminary Journal 1* (Spring 1996), 154

[99] This is an argument from silence, but seems reasonable from context. Simon is not specifically mentioned, but neither is he mentioned as not being part of the group who received the Spirit. Also he was identified with the Samaritan group earlier, and as the key character in the passage it seems that if he had been unique among the Samaritans in not receiving the Holy Spirit it would warrant mentioning in the text. Without any mention of any exception on the part of Simon we must assume that his experience was unremarkably similar to the remainder of the Samaritans.

harshness of these statements has led some interpreters to the position that Simon must not be saved. However, it is crucial to the interpretation of this passage to observe that the text says Simon believed (aorist active indicative ἐπίστευσεν) just as the other Samaritans believed (aorist active indicative ἐπίστευσαν). There are no qualifiers within the text itself that indicate that Simon's experience was any different than the other Samaritans, and therefore it seems unwise to evaluate his faith as anything other than genuine. Unless we adopt the position that none of the Samaritan believers were regenerate (and the text of verse 12 makes that position untenable), we have no textual reason to assign Simon to the status of unregenerate "professor."

To make the point even stronger, we must look closely at Luke's comment on the faith of Simon, "ὁ δὲ Σίμων καὶ αὐτὸς ἐπίστευσεν καὶ βαπτισθεὶς." Luke makes a particular point to emphasize that "*Even Simon himself* believed and was baptized." Luke gives absolutely no indicators to the exegete that this is anything other than a genuine conversion. Rather it seems just the opposite, that Luke makes great pains to point out that even this sorcerer placed faith in Christ along with the other people of Samaria. The emphatic inclusion of καὶ αὐτὸς tells us that Luke is trying to impress his reader with amazement, that even this renowned sorcerer and heathen believed the preaching of Phillip. Luke tells us in verse 12 that Phillip came "...preaching the good news about the kingdom of God and the name of Jesus Christ," and tells us that even Simon believed that message and was baptized.

The theological argument is over whether there is a difference between being a believer in Christ and a disciple of Christ, which is an argument that involves more than just this text. Even if we grant the assumption that they are the same (which we do not), Luke even tells us in verse 13 that Simon continued on with Phillip, seemingly entering into a discipleship relationship

56

with him. It seems that without any other indicators in this instance that we must conclude that Simon's experience matched the rest of the Samaritans who heard Phillip, namely that he placed faith in Christ for salvation.

Based on this analysis, the journey of Simon is best described as follows: He became a Christian, was baptized, became a disciple of Philip, sinned because of greed, and was in need of repentance and forgiveness. This analysis seems to make great sense in light of Paul's emphasis on growth in Christ and John's epistles view of the continual need for confession and repentance among believers.

Unfortunately, most commentators miss the connection of the next story that Luke provides with the same evangelist (Phillip), the same message, and the same response (belief and baptism) described in the story of the Ethiopian Eunuch.[100] Here we see Philip deliver the same message resulting in the same response as in the Samaritans and Simon: Preaching the gospel, hearing the gospel, belief in the gospel, and baptism, culminating in the vanishing evangelist.

The two stories provide a dual picture of the type of people who will respond favorably to the life giving message of Jesus. Luke provides an excellent study in contrasts. Simon is steeped in sorcery; the eunuch is steeped in the Scriptures (specifically when Phillip arrives, Isaiah). Simon is lost in his sin of magic; the eunuch is lost in his religion coming from the worship of the temple. Both need to hear and believe the life-giving message, and they both do. The dual portrait is meant to teach Theophilus (Acts 1:1-2) that the power of the gospel of Jesus can reach both the good and the bad (the ugly aren't specifically mentioned). This motif is manifested in the life of Saul (who is next up in the narrative of Acts to hear Jesus Himself preach the offer of eternal life), who is used by Luke to introduce and close out the section. The inclusion is seen in the reference to Saul 8:1, and again in 9:1   In fact Saul is a tremendous example of both the good religious eunuch bound for hell, and the evil Simon also bound for hell, as

---

[100] I (Fred) was made aware of this connection by Zane Hodges in a private discussion in 1980.

Saul himself is a worshiper and leader in the temple as well as a Christian-killer. He embodies both "the good and the bad."

As is true for Simon and the Ethiopian eunuch, the power of the gospel received simply by faith alone in Christ alone will save him. There was nothing deficient in any of their responses. It is only theological bias, not exegetical detail, which concludes they had a less-than-salvific faith. Luke tells us that we will see Simon Magus some day in heaven.

Johannine Thought

No discussion of soteriology would be adequate without an analysis of the Johannine corpus. As we saw in our lexical and grammatical analysis above John's writings are certainly at the center of the debate over the nature of faith in the New Testament. Many books and dissertations have been written on John's view of soteriology and his view of perseverance on both sides of the Lordship debate. No study of faith in the New Testament would begin to assess what it means to believe in Jesus Christ for salvation without a careful study of the Gospel of John.

It is crucial for us to exegete critical passages in John to analyze John's concept of faith. As we saw above in our grammatical and syntactical discussion, some would argue that John's use of differing tenses was deliberately employed with πιστεύω to differentiate between genuine and false professions of faith. Our analysis showed the errors in that line of thought. What of the texts themselves, though? There are several critical passages in John's gospel that lie at the center of the debate. Are the believers in John 2:23, who Jesus distrusts in 2:24, headed to hell? Are only those who are obedient and persevere in mind in 3:36? What is the eternal destiny of the rulers who were afraid to confess Christ in 12:42? Are the ones who were said to believe in Him in 8:30 still under condemnation? Only a careful analysis of the texts themselves can answer that question for us.

John 2:23-25

This text has engendered much debate and disagreement between evangelical scholars. In this passage John tells his readers of the experience of the crowds surrounding Jesus at the Passover in Jerusalem:

> Now when He was in Jerusalem at the Passover, during the feast, many believed in His name, observing His signs which He was doing. [24]But Jesus, on His part, was not entrusting Himself to them, for He knew all men, [25]and because He did not need anyone to testify concerning man, for He Himself knew what was in man. (NASB)

The main differences come from theological arguments, but we must maintain our hermeneutical spiral and evaluate the text on its own merits. The Greek text reads:

> "Ὡς δὲ ἦν ἐν τοῖς Ἱεροσολύμοις ἐν τῷ πάσχα ἐν τῇ ἑορτῇ, πολλοὶ **ἐπίστευσαν** εἰς τὸ ὄνομα αὐτοῦ θεωροῦντες αὐτοῦ τὰ σημεῖα ἃ ἐποίει· αὐτὸς δὲ Ἰησοῦς οὐκ **ἐπίστευεν** αὐτὸν αὐτοῖς διὰ τὸ αὐτὸν γινώσκειν πάντας καὶ ὅτι οὐ χρείαν εἶχεν ἵνα τις μαρτυρήσῃ περὶ τοῦ ἀνθρώπου· αὐτὸς γὰρ ἐγίνωσκεν τί ἦν ἐν τῷ ἀνθρώπῳ." (John 2:23-25)

The majority of commentators draw the conclusion that the people mentioned are unregenerate because the text tells us that Jesus literally "…was not believing in them." Some use Calvin's category of "spurious faith" for these people. Others refer to their faith as a false faith, based in Jesus' miracles rather than in His person.[101] Steve Tracy[102] finds four reasons for regarding the status of these people as unregenerate:

---

[101] See Andreas J. Kostenberger, *John* in *Baker Exegetical Commentary on the New Testament* (Grand Rapids, MI; Baker Publishing 2004), 115; D. A. Carson *The Gospel According to John* (Grand Rapids, MI, Eerdmans, 1991), 184-185; George R. Beasley-Murray, *John*, vol. 36 of *Word Biblical Commentary* (Dallas; Word, Inc., 2002), 47.

    It is amazing that Keener in his recent, massive 1650 page commentary on the gospel of John only gives 1 page concerning John 2:21-23. He fails to deal with any of the exegetical details of the text except limiting it to a transition to the Nicodemus passage, while reading in sociological/cultural speculations to determine that the audience is to be understood as unsaved,

1. The object of faith was Jesus' name and not His person.[103]

2. The foundation of the faith was the signs Jesus performed.

3. Christ's response to their faith was that He did not entrust Himself to them.

4. The purpose of 2:23-25 is to introduce the Nicodemus account. Nicodemus did not possess saving faith when he came to Jesus, and therefore by Semitic parallelism neither did the crowd of 2:23-25.

First, it is important to notice that two different forms of πιστεύω are used here. When referring to the people John uses the aorist active indicative, but for the response of Jesus he uses the imperfect active indicative. Also we must observe the full construction regarding the belief of the people: "ἐπίστευσαν εἰς τὸ ὄνομα αὐτοῦ." As part of our observation we must note that John uses this exact construction in John 1:12 to describe people who are given eternal life. Though some would point to the fact that John uses a present participle of πιστεύω in 1:12 (which they would interpret as continuing faith, in contrast to the non-continuous, aoristic faith in 2:23), we must remember that participles do not have time or aspect that is independent of the main verb (as discussed above). The main verb in 1:12 is the aorist active indicative of δίδωμι, and therefore the present participle of πιστεύω acts at the same time as the main verb[104], namely at a point of time in the past.

---

unregenerate people whom he calls "untrustworthy believers". See Craig Keener, *The Gospel of John: A Commentary* (Peabody, MA: Hendrickson Publishers, 2003), 1:531 & 1:276, 325
[102] Steve Tracy, "Models of Faith Tested Against the Gospel of John" (Th.M. diss.; Western Conservative Baptist Seminary, 1990), 53-67. This dissertation was written in 1990, and therefore we must note that his personal convictions and arguments may have changed or adapted. It is a well-written, thoughtful, and representative work that presents the classical Reformed understanding of this passage in a clear way for discussion.
[103] Tracy states that he does not believe this argument is valid. Ibid, 55 (see discussion below)
[104] This grants for the sake of discussion that aspect is present in this participle. In that the articular participle is functioning in 1:12 as a substantive, it is doubtful that the participle contains much if any view towards an aspect or *Aktionsart*. Therefore the difference in tenses

The impact of 1:12 on our interpretation of 2:23 is enormous; John uses the identical phrase of salvific belief in 1:12 that he uses in 2:23. Anderson notes, "...nothing inherent in the statement about their faith distinguishes it from the faith of others in John."[105] Hodges summarizes the point well:

> The first example of πιστεύειν εἰς τὸ ὄνομα is in the familiar salvation passage in John 1:12–13: "But as many as received him, to them gave he power to become the sons of God, even to them that believe on his name: which were born, not of blood, nor of the will of the flesh, nor of the will of man, but of God." The second Johannine usage of the phrase is in the passage under review! It is an understatement to point out that there is nothing in the usage in 1:12 that in any way prepares the reader to understand 2:23 as most commentators understand it.
>
> Even more damaging to the consensus view of 2:23 is the fact that it is expressly affirmed in 3:18 that the grounds of a man's condemnation are to be found in the fact that "he hath not believed in the name [πιστεύειν εἰς τὸ ὄνομα] of the only begotten Son of God." Moreover, in the Gospel's thematic statement in 20:31 it is declared that the believer has life "through his name" (ἐν τῷ ὀνόματι αὐτοῦ). It seems truly incredible in the light of such crucial assertions as these that John should declare in 2:23 that "many believed in His name" and at the same time should hold the opinion that those who did so did not have life and still stood under God's condemnation. Absolutely nothing in John's usage of πιστεύειν εἰς τὸ ὄνομα prepares his readers for such a conclusion.[106]

It is beyond the scope of this study to analyze the content and Old Testament backdrop of the "name" of a person, but for the purpose of this study it is sufficient to note the parallel between the requirements for adoption in 1:12 and the experience of the people in 2:23. John uses this exact phrase both before (in 1:12) and after (in 3:18) to describe genuine

---

between 1:12 and this usage is of limited exegetical significance, if any. See the discussion above regarding substantival participles and aspect.
[105] David Anderson, "The Nature of Faith", 16
[106] Zane Hodges. "Problem Passages in the Gospel of John Part II: Untrustworthy Believers-John 2:23-25" in *Bibliotheca Sacra Volume 135* (April 1978), 140-141.

conversion experiences. This fact renders extremely improbable the thought that the experience of the people in 2:23 was anything other than a genuine conversion. Anderson further notes:

> In John Chapter 3 the fourfold use of *believe in* is
> especially troubling for anyone contending that believing
> in the name of Jesus is insufficient for regeneration. Here
> Jesus explains to Nicodemus what is necessary to be born
> again, or born from above (John 3:15–16, 18, 36). In 3:18,
> Jesus specifically says the reason God will condemn a man
> is *because he has not believed in the name of the only
> begotten Son of God.* And in the thematic statement for the
> Gospel (John 20:31) John clearly declares that life comes
> "through His name."[107]

C.H. Dodd, in his work on John, finds that this phrase is, in the end analysis, a "variant" with functional identity to the phrase πιστυειν εις αυτου.[108] Tracy makes the following analysis of this phrase:

> The problem with this view [that the belief in His name
> is insufficient to save] is essentially two fold. First of all,
> given the Semitic approach to names, if one believes that
> "His name" was intended by John to mean something
> different from "Him" or "Christ," it would make more
> sense to argue that these individuals were believing in
> what the name stood for, and thus were genuine believers.
> The second problem with this view is that it does not
> take into account John's use of the phrase πιστεύω εἰς τὸ
> ὄνομα, which is found only in 1:12, 2:23, and 3:18. An
> inspection of these three passages reveals that πιστεύω
> εἰς τὸ ὄνομα is not a technical phrase which refers to the
> total person or to the character the name stood for, since
> "believe on the name" "receive" and "believe" are used in
> a parallel and interchangeable manner. Thus, for John to
> tell us "many believed on His name," he meant that many
> believed in Christ. The name of Christ simply indicates
> that Christ was the object of their faith.[109]

---

[107] David Anderson, "The Nature of Faith", 17
[108] C.H. Dodd, *The Interpretation of the Fourth Gospel* (Cambridge; University Press, 1968), 184
[109] Steve Tracy, "Models of Faith", 56

Even George Turner, himself thoroughly Reformed, places this usage of the πιστεύω εἰς formula on a par with other instances in John's gospel:

> The distinctive Johannine formula is "believe in"
> (pisteuein eis) as in 1:12; 2:23; 3:18; 4:39, 41—to mention
> a few instances. It means to believe "into" Jesus or "into"
> his name, reminiscent of the Pauline phrase "in Christ."
> This formula often alternates with "believe that" (pisteuein
> hoti) as in 11:25–27, 40, 42; 16:30. To believe "into"
> implies a personal commitment lacking in the more formal
> "believe that." It "takes the believer out of himself and
> makes him one with Christ," says Leon Morris. Like
> James, the Evangelist urges a more vital relationship than
> mere acceptance of a doctrine *about* someone or
> something (James 2:18–26).[110]

Only significant *a priori* assumptions would lead the interpreter to look for anything other than the obvious inference that these were eternally saved people. Debbie Hunn summarizes the point well:

> Certainly Jesus could not be fooled by appearance, but the
> text does not say that the people appeared to believe or that
> they spoke well-intentioned words, but that they believed
> in his name. Their faith was not spurious.[111]

The second point of contention in this passage is the reason the people believed: their faith was caused by the signs Jesus had performed. As Tracy notes, "...saving faith looks beyond the miraculous power of the wonder worker and includes trust in the one performing the signs."[112] Some commentators argue that because Jesus did not "believe" in these people, their faith must be false. If their faith was based on signs, it is argued, it must not be genuine. Tracy further explains:

> The believing of 2:23-24 as well as 3:2 is prompted by
> miraculous signs, but the salvific Christological truths
> behind the signs which was perceived and accepted in 2:11

---

[110]George Allen Turner, "Soteriology in the Gospel of John" in *Journal of the Evangelical Theological Society Volume 19*, (Fall 1976), 272.

[111] Debbie Hunn, "The Believers Jesus Doubted: John 2:23-25" in *Trinity Journal 25NS* (2004), 15-16

[112] Turner, "Soteriology", 57

now seems to be absent...The signs prompted faith which
was not yet saving. This was clearly the case with
Nicodemus in chapter three, which strengthens the
possibility of it being the case here in chapter two.[113]

There are several serious concerns with this view. These people are said
to have believed (aorist indicative – normally simple occurrence at a point in
time), and this should engender caution against evaluating how genuine their
faith is. Though the argument is made that "the salvific Christological truths
behind the signs...seems to be absent," this is an argument from silence.
John gives the reader no clue that the belief of these people was any different
than the previous or succeeding examples.

The literal translation of their belief is, "Many believed into the name of
Him." The πιστεύω εἰς construction is used here, which we have seen
normally refers to genuine salvific belief. Tracy discusses the nature of the
πιστεύω εἰς construction as being especially significant and salvific
(indicating commitment to a person in his words),[114] but then states in this
instance, "Though we would normally expect this construction of πιστεύω
to indicate saving faith, it does not in this passage."[115] This is a case of
special pleading, in that there are no other uses of πιστεύω εἰς in John's
gospel that are relegated to non-saving status in Tracy's work.

We must also recognize that the very purpose of the signs John includes
in his gospel is to elicit faith that results in eternal life. This is exactly what
happened in 2:23, which may be viewed as a Johannine paradigmatic
formula as evidenced in the purpose statement of the book in 20:30-31:

> And truly Jesus did many other signs in the presence of
> His disciples, which are not written in this book; but these
> are written that you may believe that Jesus is the Christ,
> the Son of God, and that believing you may have life in
> His name.

---

[113] Ibid, 59
[114] Ibid, 47-50
[115] Ibid, 53

The purpose of signs is to cause people to have faith in His name (i.e. in Him). The book of John is famous for the 7 signs,[116] all of which are to direct a person to faith in the son of God, which in turn results in eternal life in His name. The disciples in 2:11 seem to be a perfect precursor to these people: "This beginning of His signs Jesus did in Cana of Galilee, and manifested His glory, and His disciples believed in Him." Jesus performed signs and the disciples believed. In 2:23 Jesus did signs and the people believed.

As we have noted above, Christ was the object of the faith of the people, not the miracle-working. There is nothing in the text to indicate that the experience of the people in 2:23 is anything different than the disciples in 2:11, nor anything different than the promise of God that John makes in 1:12.

We should certainly also consider whether sign faith is commendable and worthy of receiving eternal life. In John 14:11, Jesus tells the disciples to "believe because of the works themselves." This clearly includes the signs Jesus had done. Here Jesus commands sign-based faith. Therefore there is no reason the text gives for doubting the validity of faith in Christ based on the signs He performed. Hunn succinctly summarizes the validity of sign-based faith:

> The gospel, in fact, records many coming to faith
> because of signs and contrasts them with those who did not
> believe. John 7:31 says that many believed in Jesus
> because of the number of his signs. The people strove
> with each other in their mixed opinion of Jesus following
> his healing of the lame man in ch. 5. A man born blind
> believed in Jesus because he healed him of his blindness
> (9:11, 30-38). The one man struggled to come to faith, and
> the Pharisees struggled to remain in unbelief. When Jesus
> raised Lazarus many people believed, but others planned to
> kill Jesus (11:45-53). The book is full of conflict over

---

[116] See John Niemelä, "The Message of Life in the Gospel of John", *Chafer Theological Seminary Journal 7:3* (July 2001), 3-7 for a discussion of the 7 signs. Niemelä himself espouses a view that includes an eighth sign, namely the cross and resurrection.

Jesus' signs. Those who believed in him due to the signs
truly believed, and Jesus expected this: this is what the
signs were meant to accomplish (12:37; 20:30-31).[117]

The third objection to the eternal deliverance of these people is Christ's
response to their faith. Tracy summarizes the Reformed understanding of
this point well:

> The third indicator that these individuals had not
> experienced saving faith is seen in Christ's response to
> them, for John says Christ responded to their "faith"
> (ἐπίστευσαν) by not entrusting Himself to them
> (ἐπίστευεν). The parallel verb forms used to compare the
> response of Christ to that of His followers (aorist, active,
> indicative of πιστεύω) would seem to indicate theological
> parallelism. In neither case was genuine faith or trust
> being exercised.[118]

Though Tracy makes a detailed case that intimate fellowship with Christ
is an experience in Johannine writings for all believers and not just a select
few, there seems to be a significant logical flaw with the argument above
that is overlooked.[119] Tracy calls the response of Jesus to the crowd a case
of theological parallelism, in that Jesus paralleled the reaction of the crowd
in His own reaction, neither of which was genuine trust. However, it seems
that the text gives the reader the exact opposite conclusion, namely that what
was occurring was theologically antithetical rather than parallel. The crowd
"believed" (ἐπίστευσαν), but Jesus *did not "believe"/"entrust"* (οὐκ
ἐπίστευεν). The text tells us that Jesus' reaction was the exact opposite of

---

[117] Debbie Hunn, "The Believers Jesus Doubted", 17.

[118] Ibid, 61.

[119] This does not include the grammatical error. The response of Jesus is in the imperfect, not
the aorist as he states; this does not incredibly alter the interpretation of the passage with respect
to the parallelism of the usage. However, the case is weakened by the fact that the forms are *not*
identical, and therefore not in parallel. It is possible that his argument is based upon the
parallelism of the voice and mood (active indicatives), but if that is the case his argument is a
non sequitur, in that the difference of the tenses overrides the similarities in the voice and mood.
In fact, it would seem that just the opposite is in view: Jesus' response to the crowd lies *in
contrast* to their response to Him (as seen in the aspectual difference between the aorist and
imperfect).

the crowds'. Since clearly Jesus did not trust the crowd, the only logical explanation the text offers the exegete is that the crowd did exactly the opposite of what Jesus did, namely entrust themselves to Him. The argument that Jesus' reaction is identical to the *true* intent of the crowd cannot be supported from the words of the text.

Lastly, the rhetorical or literary role of 2:23-24 must be considered. Again, Tracy provides a salient representation of the Reformed understanding of the role of the passage:

> The fourth and final indicator that these individuals had not experienced saving faith is seen in the manner in which this section serves to introduce the Nicodemus account. The more one studies the fourth Gospel, the more apparent it becomes that John was an amazingly skillful and artistic narrator, who was purposeful in the inclusion of every single portion of his gospel. It is widely agreed that 2:23-25 serves structurally as a transition and introduction to the Nicodemus account. The introductory nature of 2:23-25 is seen in the parallels of the two sections. In both we have: Jews in Jerusalem who were at least sympathetic to Christ, whose faith was rooted in the miraculous, who were internally examined by Christ, whose faith was said to be deficient.
> Everyone agrees that Nicodemus did not possess saving faith when he came to Christ in the night, so it is quite reasonable to conclude in light of the other parallels, that the individuals in 2:23-25 were also not regenerate. This interpretation also gives a more logical explanation for the inclusion of 2:23-25. In typically Jewish fashion the story or principle is given in summary form first (2:23-25), and then is retold in more detail.[120]

It is readily agreed that John was indeed "an amazingly skillful and artistic narrator, who was purposeful in the inclusion of every single portion of his gospel." It seems in this instance, though, the exegete would be better served to look within the gospel itself for the Johannine interaction between the responses of the crowd and the Pharisees to Jesus, rather than appealing to Semitic parallelism. Pharisees are expressly mentioned 20 times in John's

---

[120] Ibid, 66-67

gospel,[121] and with the exception of 18:13 (where the use merely identifies the source of the guards who came for Jesus in Gethsemane), every passage *contrasts* the response of the crowds and the Pharisees:

- 1:19-25: John is baptizing; the people respond but the Pharisees question
- 2:23-3:21: The crowds believe; Nicodemus (a Pharisee) is skeptical
- 4:1-4: Jesus' disciples were baptizing more than John (i.e. the crowd was responding to Jesus), and once the Pharisees heard Jesus left Judea
- 7:31-32: The crowd believes in Him, but the Pharisees sent officers to seize Him
- 7:40-52: The crowds respond to Jesus, and the Pharisees make sure none of the rulers or priests have believed in Him
- 8:1-11: Jesus teaches the people, and the Pharisees cause a disturbance by accusing an adulteress (the text here is doubtful)
- 8:12-30: Jesus speaks to the crowd; many believe in Him (v. 30), but the Pharisees judge Jesus' testimony as false (v. 13)
- 9:13-41: The healed blind man is accosted by the Pharisees over Jesus' healing of him
- 11:45-57: Many of the Jews came to Mary and because of the testimony believed in Him. This causes the Pharisees to plot to kill Jesus
- 12:17-19: the people testify to the greatness of Jesus, but the Pharisees get frustrated at His rise in popularity

---

[121] 1:24; 3:1; 4:1; 7:32 (twice), 45, 47, 48; 8:3; 8:13; 9:13, 15, 16, 40; 11:46, 47, 57; 12:19, 42; 18:3

- 12:42: Even some of the rulers believed, but were afraid of the reaction of the Pharisees.

Unless this section is a sole exception (which again would be a case of special pleading) John's clear and consistent contrast between the response of the people and the Pharisees must guide our interpretation here. Our analysis of John's contrast of the crowds and the Pharisees shows us that, logically, John is again setting the dullness and rejection of the religious establishment (as exemplified in the Pharisees) over against the belief and acceptance of the common people. Since the best analysis of the Nicodemus account is that Nicodemus at this point had not accepted Christ,[122] the only logical conclusion the exegete can draw is that the crowd, by way of contrast, did believe and were therefore regenerate people.

The primary statement in the passage seems to be the response of Jesus. The imperfect most often caries an inceptive force,[123] referring to something that was beginning to happen. Here it is best translated, "But Jesus was not entrusting himself to them because he knew all men." There is no reason to say that this was a permanent state of mind; all the text tells us is that Jesus was not yet ready to commit Himself to their care. It seems apparent that Jesus was not entrusting himself to these people yet, because their faith was infantile and weak. Jesus would not entrust His security in Judea to people whom He knew would eventually leave Him.[124] It was not the kind of faith that was mature enough to be trustworthy yet, but this does not mean it was

---

[122] At a later point in John's gospel Nicodemus does seem to be presented as a believer alongside of Joseph of Arimathea, another "secret" disciple of Jesus (John 19:38-39).

[123] See Daniel Wallace, *Greek Grammar*, 540-552 for a discussion of the various nuances of the imperfect. On 544 he states that the ingressive/inceptive imperfect is possibly the most common imperfect in narrative, which strengthens the interpretation presented here. None of the other options for the imperfect discussed by Wallace (with the possible exception of the descriptive/progressive imperfect, which is nearly the same as the inceptive) seem to make sense of this use.

[124] See Debbie Hunn, "The Believers Jesus Doubted", 18-20 for a discussion on trusting someone for safety as an acceptable part of the semantic range of πιστεύω. Her analysis confirms the fact that in this instance John has the idea of personal safety in mind, and that this idea fits John's usages as well as the semantic range of πιστεύω.

not genuine faith.[125] To ask the question "Do you have Christian friends that you do not fully trust" is to answer it.

In light of the evidence from the text of John 2:23-25, it seems we must consider the faith of the people to be genuine, and also conclude that they are eternally saved individuals whose faith was immature and unreliable. Even the most staunchly Reformed scholars agree that believers in Christ require time and discipleship to mature and have a tested, trustworthy walk with Christ. The believers of John 2:23-25 had not yet matured to the point of being trustworthy, and therefore Jesus was not yet ready to entrust Himself to them. Their infantile faith, though, is no cause for the exegete to doubt its validity, and after thorough examination the evidence strongly points to the conclusion that the people in 2:23-25 experienced genuine conversion.

John 3:36

Especially in light of the argument presented in the syntactical section above concerning πιστεύω and πείθω, it is imperative to consider John 3:36. Both terms are present (if we consider ἀπειθέω the negative of πείθω), with πείθω being the source of contention. The text reads:

"ὁ **πιστεύων** εἰς τὸν υἱὸν ἔχει ζωὴν αἰώνιον· ὁ δὲ **ἀπειθῶν** τῷ υἱῷ οὐκ ὄψεται ζωήν, ἀλλ᾽ ἡ ὀργὴ τοῦ θεοῦ μένει ἐπ᾽ αὐτόν."

Lordship proponents interpret John 3:36 as an example of parallelism, where obedience is seen as a synonym for faith. This builds from the argument, discussed above, regarding the common root for πιστεύω and πείθω. It is argued from that logic, as well as from this instance, that "belief" is synonymous or near-synonymous with "obedience" and therefore

---

[125] This is also seen in Paul commenting on the danger of shipwrecked faith or of a faith that can be overturned or made weak. See below for a discussion on 1 Tim 1:8-9 and the nature of shipwrecked faith.

saving faith is obedient faith.[126] They would point to the definition of πείθω

in BDAG to strengthen their argument that we should not assign the

definition of "disbelieve" to ἀπειθῶν: "In a number of pass. NRSV and

REB, among others, with less probability render ἀ[πειθέω] 'disbelieve' or

equivalent."[127]

However, from context it can be determined that ἀπειθέω in this instance

may be rendered as "disbelieving." As above in the discussion of πιστεύω,

it appears that Danker made a significant change to the definition of

ἀπειθέω in BDAG without additional warrant or evidence. In BAGD, the

entry reads:

> "...since, in the view of the early Christians, the
> supreme disobedience was a refusal to believe
> their gospel, ἀπειθέω may be restricted in some
> passages to the meaning *disbelieve, be an
> unbeliever*. This sense, though greatly disputed (it
> is not found outside our literature), seems most
> probable in J 3:36; Ac 14:2; 19:9; Ro 15:31, and
> only slightly less probable in Ro 2:8; 1 Pt 2:8;
> 3:1, perhaps also vs. 20; 4:17; IMg 8:2.[128]

Danker appears to have made the change in BDAG without providing any

additional lexical evidence to support the change. Makidon points this out:

> Yet, John 3:36 and Acts 14:2 clearly juxtapose belief and
> disobedience (disbelief). Acts 19:9 has a clear contrast as well.
> Luke writes,
>> And he [Paul] went into the synagogue and spoke
>> boldly for three months, *reasoning* and *persuading*
>> concerning the things of the kingdom of God. But
>> when some were *hardened* and did *not believe*
>> [ēpeithoun], but spoke evil of the Way before the

---

[126] See Fred Chay, "The Danger of Neo Legalism: An Assessment of the Theology of Norman Shepherd, Daniel Fuller, John Piper, Thomas Schriener, and Paul Rainbow Concerning the Nature of Faith" Also see John Piper, *Future Grace,* 34,43, 162 and Daniel Fuller, *Unity of the Bible,* 301ff

[127] BDAG, s.v. "ἀπειθέω," page 99

[128] BAGD, s.v. "ἀπειθέω," 82

> multitude, he departed from them and withdrew the
> disciples, reasoning daily in the school of Tyrannus
> (Acts 19:8–9, emphasis added).

Luke's two contrasts are clearly evident (reasoning/hardened
and persuading/disbelieving). If one will not respond to
reasoning, he is *hardened.* If one will not be *persuaded,* he is
disbelieving (disobedient to the message of eternal life).[129]

Seen in this light, with the backing of BAGD as well as Moulton and

Milligan, it seems it is unwise to bring a definition of obedience into the

semantic range of πιστεύω in John 3:36. It seems, then, that BAGD has

made the correct assessment as opposed to BDAG. Context indicates, in

light of the clear theme in John 3 of the difference between belief and

unbelief, that the disobedience in mind in 3:36 is a refusal to be persuaded to

believe. Building from the definition of πείθω of "to cause to come to a

particular point of view," it can be seen that those who are ἀπειθῶν are those

who have not been persuaded to believe in Christ and be saved. Thus they

are unbelievers, with the supreme disobedience being unbelief. John 3:36,

then, is best viewed as describing "the obedience that is faith" or "the

obedience required is to obey the command to believe" rather than "faith

means obedience."

John 12:42-43

This passage is regarded by some[130] as a marker of people who exercised

false or insufficient faith:

> Nevertheless many even of the rulers believed in Him, but
> because of the Pharisees they were not confessing Him, for
> fear that they would be put out of the synagogue; for they
> loved the approval of men rather than the approval of God.
> (John 12:42-43)

---

[129]Michael Makidon, "Soteriological Concerns with Bauer's Greek Lexicon," 17

[130] For instance, see James E. Rosscup, "The Overcomer of the Apocalypse" in *Grace
Theological Journal Volume 3*(Fall 1982), 270

The argument for false faith in this passage stems from the fact that immediately after the authorities believed, they did not "confess Him." Some theologians would point to Romans 10:9-10 as evidence that this non-confessing faith is non-salvific from a position that failure to confess Jesus as Lord of a person's life is evidence of an unregenerate heart (this passage will be discussed below). However, the discussion of John 2:23 above bears on this passage as well. The text at hand reads:

> "ὅμως μέντοι καὶ ἐκ τῶν ἀρχόντων πολλοὶ **ἐπίστευσαν εἰς αὐτόν**, ἀλλὰ διὰ τοὺς Φαρισαίους οὐχ ὡμολόγουν ἵνα μὴ ἀποσυνάγωγοι γένωνται" (John 12:42)

Once again the aorist indicative verb occurs with a participial direct object clause. As was discussed above, "believing into Him" is a Johannine formula for a person receiving eternal life. This phrase is found only in John's Gospel, and is found there 7 times (2:11; 4:39; 7:31; 8:30; 10:42; 11:45; 12:42). Every other instance is unambiguous in attesting to people having salvific faith in Jesus Christ. It would seem, then, that this phrase would have to be a significant exception within the Gospel of John if it were referring to false faith. Every other instance in John is eternally salvific, and there is no contextual indicator that John provides the reader to indicate that he is intending these people to be seen as an exception to his otherwise unified use of the phrase. Anderson makes this helpful insight:

> There is no contextual indication that these rulers were false professors. Here we have the same Greek expression used by John to indicate a personal relationship with Christ: ἐπίστευσαν εἰς αὐτόν [*believed in Him*]. These rulers were born-again believers, but because of their fear (not of death, but of losing synagogue privileges), they were unwilling to identify openly with Jesus.
> In addition, remember Nicodemus who came to Jesus *by night*? He was a *ruler* (ἄρχων) *of the Jews*, the same term applied to those who believed in Jesus in John 12:42. Could it be that Nicodemus was one of these *men* who believed in 2:23 because he saw the signs, but was still

73

unwilling to identify openly with Him because he was a
ruler of the Jews and would be expelled from the
synagogue? Given the context, it is likely.[131]

In light of these facts, it seems that we must reject the position that these
men are unregenerate. The phrase John uses in 12:42 to describe their state
matches his use elsewhere in his Gospel for genuine conversion *without
exception.* What, then, are we to make of their lack of confidence in Christ
before men? It is important to consider that just as children are not born full
grown, neither are new Christians born full grown. The numerous
exhortations in the epistles to be strong in Christ and grow in Him bear
witness to the truth that this is a process rather than an event. It is possible to
believe and yet not be fully comfortable with or even aware of all of the
ramifications of the decision. Fear was a perfectly normal reaction for these
men considering the high cost for traitors to Judaism.

At a literary level we should notice that one of the sub-themes of the
gospel of John is the function of "abiding". This is not the same as receiving
eternal life. The concept of abiding is seen with Jesus and His disciples in
the upper room discourse (John 13-17). There is a clear distinction between
the condition and the consequences of believing to receive eternal life and
the need to abide in Christ with the consequence of the Father and the Son
deepening their relationship to the disciples. (John 14:21)

It is important to notice that there is an inversion of topic and emphasis
between First John and the Gospel of John. In the gospel the central issue is
how to receive eternal life, with only a subplot of developing intimacy with
Jesus. In the letter of First John the two topics are reversed in proportions.
First John focuses on how to abide in Christ with only a portion of the letter
given over to how to gain eternal life. This is somewhat based on ones view
of the purpose of the book of First John that is legendary in its debate.[132]

---

[131] David Anderson, "The Nature of Faith", 24

[132] The purpose statement of 1 John is most naturally found at 1 John 1:3, "what we have seen
and heard we proclaim to you also, so that you too may have fellowship with us; and indeed our

But the issue has to do with the sub-plot of developing courage and the resulting intimacy with Jesus in the Gospel of John.

The main characters for this are Nicodemus and Joseph of Arimathea. Nicodemus came to Jesus at night out of fear of the Pharisees. The last report of Nicodemus, the famous Pharisee is that he shows up with Joseph in the day to claim the body of Jesus. The important issue is that Joseph is called "a secret disciple of Jesus." (John 19:38) He was hiding in secret until at last he had the courage to come out into the light with Nicodemus to reveal their shared commitment to Christ. The illustration of John 12 and of those who were afraid to confess Christ in the open, even though the text says "they believed in Him," is obviously to be seen in counter-distinction to Joseph's courage in the final hour.

Though we would not commend it, certainly we should not sit in judgment from the comfort and ease of 21st century America over people in fear of their very lives. Furthermore it is entirely possible to believe in Christ, and yet still enjoy prestige and the favor of men. It seems, then, that the best interpretation of this passage is that these men genuinely believed in Christ, but were immature and needed discipleship and maturity. The progression of discipleship in the cases of Nicodemus and Joseph of Arimathea, along with the lexical and grammatical evidence, leads us to the conclusion that the faith of the "secret disciples' of John 12:42 was genuine and salvific.

John 8:30-32

Our final passage in John has tied even some of the greatest thinkers in Christendom in knots. The passage reads:

---

fellowship is with the Father, and with His Son Jesus Christ." As Stephen S. Smalley says in *1, 2, 3 John* in *Word Biblical Commentary Volume 51* (Dallas; Word, Inc., 2002), xxviii: "The purpose of 1 John may therefore be summarized as *primarily* an appeal to the faithful: to strengthen the faith and resolve of true believers in the Johannine community by encouraging them to maintain the apostolic gospel."

[30]As He spoke these things, many came to believe in Him.
[31]So Jesus was saying to those Jews who had believed
Him, "If you continue in My word, then you are truly
disciples of Mine; [32]and you will know the truth, and the
truth will make you free."

The issue comes as John continues the section in verse 33 and beyond.

Verse 33 states, "They answered Him, "We are Abraham's descendants and

have never yet been enslaved to anyone; how is it that You say, 'You will

become free'?" This follow-on statement has led to some varied and

interesting interpretations. John said in verse 30 that πολλοὶ ἐπίστευσαν

εἰς αὐτόν. However, it seems the later response is less than receptive to the

message of Jesus. No less a scholar than John Calvin declared,

> "Though the Jews, at that time, almost resembled a dry
> and barren soil, yet God did not permit the seed of his
> word to be entirely lost. Thus, contrary to all hopes, and
> amidst so many obstructions, some fruit appears. But the
> Evangelist **inaccurately** gives the name of *faith* to that
> which was only a sort of preparation for *faith*. For he
> affirms nothing higher concerning them than that they
> were disposed to receive the doctrine of Christ, to which
> also the preceding warning refers."[133] (italics original, bold
> mine)

Some commentators differentiate between the wording in verse 30 and

verse 31. In verse 30 John says that "many came to believe in Him" (πολλοὶ

ἐπίστευσαν εἰς αὐτόν), using the πιστεύω εἰς construction discussed in

the grammatical discussion above. In verse 31, though, John uses πιστεύω

plus the dative (πεπιστευκότας αὐτῷ). Boice comments:

> To understand what the Lord Jesus Christ is saying in these verses and to
> apply them properly, we need first to understand that there is a great deal of
> difference between merely believing Jesus and believing *in* Him or *on*
> Him.[134]

---

[133] John Calvin, trans. William Pringle, *A Commentary on the Gospel According to John* (Grand Rapids, MI; Baker Books, reprint 1981), 340
[134] James Montgomery Boice, *The Gospel of John* (Grand Rapids, MI; Zondervan, 1985), 543

Jesus' words were directed not to those who had believed properly, but rather to those who had believed only on the inadequate, intellectual level.[135]

Some scholars avoid the grammatical issue, but take issue with Jesus' further discussion as indicative that the faith of these Jews was soteriologically inadequate. Keener comments:

> Yet in this instance, though many responded to Jesus with faith (8:30), it was a faith that would not persevere (8:31, 48, 59). Their failure to "abide" (8:31) suggests that they were not "sons" (8:35)...[136]

However, there are several good reasons to view the faith of these people as genuine. As discussed above in the discussion of grammatical issues and πιστεύω, the distinction between πιστεύω εἰς and πιστεύω plus the dative is nonexistent. John uses πιστεύω plus the dative in many places (2:22; 4:21, 50; 5:24, 38, 46, 47; 8:45, 46; 10:37, 38; 12:38; 14:11; the instances in chapter 5 are clearly effectively soteriological), so to set up a distinction between those who "believed in Him" and those who "believed Him" is a misuse of the grammar. As Carson reminds us in this instance, "...the linguistic distinction does not stand up."[137] Therefore it seems best to see the descriptions in verse 30 and 31 as referring to the same group.

If their faith is indeed genuine, what then of the opposition to Jesus' teaching in verse 33 and beyond? George R. Beasley-Murray provides this helpful insight into the identity of the objectors in verse 33:

> We should recognize that there is not a hint in vv 30–32 that the faith of the believers is inadequate or insincere. By contrast the would-be murderers of Jesus are told in v 37, "My word οὐ χωρεῖ ἐν ὑμῖν," which means that it has not begun to penetrate their minds (see Schnackenburg, 490 n. 82); their unbelief makes them wholly resistant to the word of Jesus. Hence in v 43 they are said to be incapable of "giving heed" to his word. After the depiction of people becoming believers in vv 30–32, the entire passage is

---

[135] Ibid, 545
[136] Craig S. Keener, *The Gospel of John*, 1:746
[137] D.A. Carson, *The Gospel According to John*, 346

punctuated by objections to faith in Jesus—vv 33, 41, 48, 52, 57. Since the objectors in the last three passages are termed "the Jews," i.e., Jewish opponents of Jesus, it is reasonable to assume that they are the protesters also in vv 33 and 41. In that case we are presented in 8:30–59 with a typical statement of Jews coming to faith in Jesus; they are instructed by him as to what true discipleship means, and there follows a mass of typical Jewish propaganda calculated to destroy faith in Jesus.[138]

Beasley-Murray helps us see that a rhetorical analysis of this passage clears up the ambiguity of the referent of the verb ἀπεκρίθησαν that begins verse 33. John carefully sets up a limiter to Jesus' audience in verse 31 with the phrase τοὺς πεπιστευκότας αὐτῷ; in verse 33 Jesus is again attacked by those Jews who remain antagonistic to Jesus and scornful of that section of the Jews who had placed faith in Christ. Charles Bing sums up the merits of this understanding of this position:

> This interpretation is most reasonable because it prevents Christ, who says in v 45 "you do not believe Me," from contradicting John, who said they "believed in Him" and "believed Him" (vv 30–31). It also has greater exegetical and theological consistency than that view which would say these are "believers who did not really believe."[139]

Jesus taught an antagonistic crowd beginning in 8:12, and His words were so persuasive that even among these people many came to believe in Him. To those who had believed, still mixed among the throng of people who wanted nothing to do with Christ, Jesus gave instructions on continuing in His word. The antagonistic element objects in verse 33, and the remainder of Jesus' comments are directed at the antagonizers and not at those who had believed in Him. Thus the faith of these people is as genuine as the faith that we have examined throughout the gospel of John. Most commentators argue

---

[138] George R. Beasley-Murray, *John*, 132-33
[139] Charles C. Bing, "The Cost of Discipleship" in *Journal of the Grace Evangelical Society Volume 6* (Spring 1993), 50

that the faith of these people fits in the same category as the faith of those in John 2:23[140], and their assessment is in the end correct. As the above analysis of 2:23 and the current discussion of 8:30-33 shows, both groups must be viewed as genuinely regenerate.

Synthesis of Johannine Passages:

By analyzing several of the most significant passages in the gospel of John it has become apparent that when John says that a person or group of people believed in Christ, then we must take him at his word and consider them regenerate. At this point it is clear that for John there exist on many levels truly regenerate people who Jesus does not trust (2:23-24), who need further instruction and encouragement (8:30-32), and who are afraid to publicly identify with Christ for fear of loss of social prestige or position (12:42). In John's writings there is a unified witness that these people are regenerate, bound for heaven when they die.

Upon close examination the only reason we can maintain that the believers in the passages discussed above are not genuine is an *a priori* commitment to perseverance theology. Textual analysis and careful exegesis have led us to the conclusion that in the gospel of John there are many instances of genuine believers who do not fit our sanctification models or preferences. Not every regenerate person in John's gospel persevered.

Pauline Corpus

The Pauline writings undoubtedly provide the clearest and most strident discussion in the entire Bible on the simplicity and clarity of the gospel message. His vehemence in his defense of the gospel of grace can be most clearly seen in the introduction to Galatians:

> But even if we, or an angel from heaven, should preach to
> you a gospel contrary to what we have preached to you, he
> is to be accursed! As we have said before, so I say again

---

[140] For instance, see D.A. Carson, *John*, 345; Craig Keener, *John*, 746.

now, if any man is preaching to you a gospel contrary to
what you received, he is to be accursed! (Gal 1:8-9)

What is the gospel that Paul preaches? As our discussion to this point has

shown, there are those who would say that Paul's gospel assumed

commitment and obedience as an intrinsic part of the gospel message. Many

argue from Paul's statements about obedience to the gospel, and to

confessing Jesus as κύριος, that Paul's understanding of conversion involves

ongoing sanctification.

We must, then, follow the same procedure we utilized for the Johannine

writings. We must analyze the critical passages used by commentators on

both sides of the Lordship debate. We must be careful and thorough in our

analysis in an attempt to ascertain Paul's view of the requirements for

conversion.

Romans 1:5

The Book of Romans contains bracketing statements concerning "the

obedience of faith" in both 1:5 and 16:26 that form an inclusio for the entire

book. John Calvin asserts in this regard that "one of the first elements of

faith is reconciliation implied in man's drawing near to God" and that "with

the heart man believeth unto righteousness."[141] His explanation of

"obedience of faith" is as follows:

> There is one consideration which ought at once to put
> an end to the debate – viz. that assent itself (as I have
> already observed, and will afterwards more fully illustrate)
> is more a matter of the heart than the head, of the affection
> than the intellect. For this reason, it is termed "obedience
> of faith" (Rom. i. 5), which the Lord prefers to all other
> service, and justly, since nothing is more precious to him
> than his truth, which, as John the Baptist declares, is in a
> manner signed and sealed by believers (John iii. 33). As
> there can be no doubt on the matter, we in one word
> conclude, that they talk absurdly when they maintain that

---

[141] John Calvin, *Institutes of the Christian Religion* 3:2:8, trans. Henry Beveridge (Grand
Rapids, MI; Eerdmans, 1989), 476.

faith is formed by the addition of pious affection as an accessory to assent, since assent itself, such at least as the Scripture describes, consists in pious affection. But we are furnished with a still clearer argument. Since faith embraces Christ as he is offered by the Father, and he is offered not only for justification, for forgiveness of sins and peace, but also for sanctification, as the fountain of living waters, it is certain that no man will ever know him aright without at the same time receiving the sanctification of his Spirit; or, to express the matter more plainly, faith consists in the knowledge of Christ; Christ cannot be known without the sanctification of his Spirit: therefore faith cannot possibly be disjoined from pious affection.[142]

Calvin further illustrates the relation between faith and obedience as follows:

Hence, Paul designates faith as the obedience which is given to the Gospel (Rom. 1:5); and writing to the Philippians, he commends them for the obedience of faith (Phil. 2:17). For faith includes not merely the knowledge that God is, but also, nay chiefly, a perception of his will towards us. It concerns us to know not only what he is in himself, but also in what character he is pleased to manifest to us. We now see, therefore, that faith is the knowledge of the divine will in regard to us, as ascertained from his word. And the foundation of it is a previous persuasion of the truth of God.[143]

The text reads δι' οὗ ἐλάβομεν χάριν καὶ ἀποστολὴν εἰς ὑπακοὴν πίστεως ἐν πᾶσιν τοῖς ἔθνεσιν ὑπὲρ τοῦ ὀνόματος αὐτοῦ.

The significant issue with this text involves the phrase εἰς ὑπακοὴν πίστεως, "into the obedience of faith."

---

[142] Ibid. Calvin seems to view assent as including pious affection. This indicates that the volitional aspect is included. Some see this fitting into the threefold definition of faith : *noticia, assensus, and fiducia*, for example, per Louis Berkhof, *Systematic Theology* (Grand Rapids, MI; Eerdmans, 1996) 503-506. However, others recoil from this automatic triad. See Gordon Clark, *What is Saving Faith?*, v-vii, 28-45; See in its entirety: R. T. Kendall, *Calvin and English Calvinism to 1649* (Oxford: Oxford University Press, 1979). For opposing views, see the following: Paul Helm, *Calvin and the Calvinists* (Carlisle, Pa.: The Banner of Truth Trust, 1982), 1-12; Walter E. Stuerman, "A Critical Study of Calvin's Concept of Faith" (Ph.D. diss., University of Tulsa, 1952), 163-175, 199-230.
[143] Ibid, 3:2:6, 474.

There are many interpretive options to the texts. First, it may be that "obedience to the faith" refers to faith that obeys – that all who believe in Christ obey God. This view takes the noun "faith" essentially and functionally as the "subject" of the verbal noun "obedience." Hence, faith obeys. This could refer to absolute obedience (sinless perfectionism), to characteristic obedience, or even to occasional obedience. However, most who hold this understanding adopt the characteristic obedience understanding. According to this view there is no sharp distinction between evangelism and discipleship. To be saved, people must produce lives that are characterized by obedience. While temporary moments of disobedience may occur, the overall pattern of life is holy.

John Murray wrote the following concerning this expression:

> "Hence, the implications of this expression 'obedience of faith' are far-reaching. For the faith which apostleship was intended to promote was not an evanescent (i.e., quickly fading) act of emotion but the commitment of whole-hearted devotion to Christ and the truth of his gospel."[144]

John MacArthur similarly comments: "Faith is by nature turned and toned toward obedience . . . so good works are inevitable in the life of one who truly believes."[145]

A second view would hold that "obedience to the faith" may refer to obeying the teachings of Scripture. In this understanding, "faith" is essentially and functionally the "object" of the verbal noun "obedience." Paul was trying to get Gentiles to obey the faith. If "the faith" is understood to refer to all of the teachings of the Christian faith, then discipleship is in view. Commentator J. P. Lange writes:

> An Epistle, sent to Rome by the ambassador of a Lord and King, who declared himself appointed to call all the peoples of the Roman Empire to obedience or allegiance,

---

[144] John Murray, *Romans* in *The New International Commentary on the New Testament*, ed. F. F. Bruce, 2 vols. in 1 (Grand Rapids, MI; Eerdmans, 1965), 13-14.

[145] John F. MacArthur, *Faith Works*, 142.

must have been planned in full consciousness of the antithesis, as well as of the analogy, between the earthly Roman Empire and the Kingdom of Christ. Therefore, the Apostle expresses the analogy when he characterizes himself as an ambassador who appeals to the nations to be obedient to his Lord. But the antithesis lies in his denoting this obedience as an obedience to the faith."[146]

Robert Govett appears to hold this view as well, though his wording allows for the possibility that he might hold some form of this first view. He says, "The receivers by faith of the message are to obey it. For with the gospel go forth commands. Faith is to show itself by obedience."[147]

A final view of the "obedience to the faith" is that this activity refers to believing the Gospel. This view understands "the faith" to refer to "the Gospel message." Grammatically, this view is arrived at either by seeing "the faith" as the object of "obedience" or by seeing "faith" as in apposition to obedience; hence, it would be translated, "the obedience that is faith." Thus, in this view, the obedience in question is obedience to the Gospel message. Anders Nygren writes, "One receives in faith that which God proffers us through Christ. This is 'the obedience of faith.' Paul is aware that he is to bring the Gentiles thereto."[148] Similarly, Zane Hodges comments:

> "An expression like 'obedience to the faith' (Rom. 1:5;
> 16:26) has nothing to do with works that follow salvation.
> Naturally, God demands that men place faith in His Son
> and is angry with them when they do not (John 3:36).
> Faith is an obedient response to the summons of the
> Gospel. But, the man who exercises faith is reaching out
> for the unconditional grace of God."[149]

---

[146] J. P. Lange and F. R. Fay, *Lange's Commentary on the Holy Scriptures,* vol. 5, "The Epistle of Paul to the Romans" (Grand Rapids, MI: Zondervan Publishing House, 1960), 63.

[147] Robert Govett, *Govett on Romans* (Hayesville, N.C.: Schoettle Publishing Company, 1981), 4. Govett, although he held a M.A. degree from Oxford University and was made a lifetime Fellow, found his views concerning eschatology regarded as unacceptable in certain theological circles. However, C. H. Spurgeon said Govett was a man who wrote one-hundred years before his time.

[148] Anders Nygren, *Commentary on Romans* (Philadelphia: Fortress Press, 1949), 55.

[149] Zane Hodges, *The Gospel Under Siege,* 2nd ed. (Dallas: Redencion Viva, 1992), 105-106.

D.B. Garlington seeks to finesse this phrase by attempting to show

that Paul meant both an appositional and possessional idea. He says:

> In Rom 1:5; 16:26 Paul has chosen to coin an
> *ambiguous* phrase which expresses two ideas at the same
> time: the obedience which consists in faith and the
> obedience which is the product of faith.[150]

However, even Garlington, who will argue strongly that the overriding

sense and import of the phrase consists in a Reformed understanding of

"believing obedience," notes that the view that commands the most respect

from commentators is the genitive of apposition, "The obedience that

consists in faith."[151] Further, in his analysis Garlington violates the principle

of single meaning that is the very bedrock of Protestant grammatical-

historical hermeneutics. As Bernard Ramm states:

> But here we must remember the old adage:
> 'Interpretation is one, application is many.' This means
> that there is only one meaning to a passage of Scripture
> which is defined by careful study.[152]

As Robert Wilkin has noted, the context is the key to a proper

interpretation:

> All we have in both places is a bare expression without
> explanation. Nothing in the immediate context suggests
> that all believers always had wholehearted devotion to
> Christ and that they are always set on obeying God. In
> fact, other passages in Romans clearly contradict this. In
> other places in Romans, Paul exhorts believers to obey
> God and holds open the possibility that they might not.
> "Shall we continue in sin that grace may abound?" (Rom.
> 6:1) "Do not let sin reign in your mortal bodies, that you
> should obey its lusts." (Rom. 6:12) "I beseech you,
> therefore, brethren, by the mercies of God, that you present

---

[150] D.B. Garlington, "The Obedience of Faith in the Letter to the Romans Part I: The meaning of ὑπακοὴ πίστεως (Rom 1:5; 16:26)", *Westminster Theological Journal 52:2* (Fall 1990), 223-224

[151] Ibid, 207

[152] Bernard Ramm, *Protestant Biblical Interpretation: A Textbook on Hermeneutics*, 3rd rev. ed. (Grand Rapids, MI; Baker Books, 1970), 113 as quoted by Robert Thomas, "The Principle of Single Meaning" in *The Master's Seminary Journal 12/1* (Spring 2001), 33-34.

your bodies a living sacrifice, holy, acceptable to God, which is your reasonable service. And do not be conformed to this world, but be transformed by the renewing of your mind." (Rom. 12:1-2) And, "Let us walk properly, as in the day, not in revelry and drunkenness, not in lewdness and lust, not in strife and envy." (Rom. 13:13)[153]

Romans 1:5 does not teach that saving faith always results in ongoing obedience to God; rather, it merely says that whenever anyone trusts in Christ for eternal life, he has obeyed God's command to do that. Wilkin continues concerning the contextual issue:

> Therefore, the decisive factor in understanding what Paul meant is in parallel passages. While there are no other passages in the New Testament which use this exact expression (other than Rom. 16:26 which is equally vague), there are quite a few which use nearly the same expression. These parallel passages refer to believing the Gospel.
> Paul linked "obedience" and "the Gospel" elsewhere in Romans, "They have not all obeyed the gospel." (Rom. 10:16) Possibly the closest parallel to Rom. 1:5 is Rom. 15:18-20. There Paul indicates that Christ has sent him to make the Gentiles "obedient" and so he concludes that "I have made it my aim to preach the gospel." Likewise, in 2 Thess. 1:8, Paul referred to unbelievers as "those who do not obey the gospel of our Lord Jesus Christ."
> In addition, many other New Testament passages outside of Paul's writings refer to faith as an act of obedience to God's command to trust in Christ. In referring to the growth of the early church, Luke—Paul's traveling companion and fellow minister of the Gospel— wrote in Acts 6:7 that "many of the priests were obedient to the faith." That, of course, is almost the exact expression Paul used in Rom. 1:5. Luke was referring to that summary statement to the fact that many Jewish priests obeyed God's command to believe the Gospel.
> John 3:36 says, "He who believes the son has eternal life; but he who does not obey the Son shall not see life, but the wrath of God abides on Him." Here disobeying the

---

[153] Much of the preceding discussion is from Robert Wilkin, *Grace Evangelical Society Newsletter,* vol. 8, no. 4 "The Obedience of Faith" (July 1993).

Son is clearly the opposite of believing Him. In other words, disbelief is an act of disobedience. The apostle Peter made this same contract: "Therefore, to you who believe, He is precious; but to those who are disobedient, 'The stone which the builders rejected has become the chief cornerstone.'" (1 Peter 2:7) Similarly, Peter spoke of believing the Gospel as "obeying the Truth" in I Peter 1:22.[154]

Faith is the act of understanding and accepting as true a proposition. In terms of the Christian faith, the gospel needs to be understood and accepted as true. When that happens then one has received the gospel or believed the truth (John 1:12) that grants a person the gift of eternal life. Grammatically the genitive of apposition makes simplest and best sense of Paul's argument, which commends it[155]. Robert Thomas' warning is appropriate for the scholar studying this passage:

Evangelicals today are drifting on the sea of uncertainty and conjecture because of their neglect of foundational principles of the grammatical-historical method of interpretation. They have become sophisticated in analyzing hermeneutical theory, but in that process have seemingly forgotten simple principles that exegetical giants of the past have taught. They are currently reaping the harvest of confusion that neglect of the past has brought upon them.[156]

By maintaining Wilkin's careful consideration of context in analysis, and avoiding Garlington's error of violating the principle of single meaning, we arrive here at the view that the genitive of apposition is the best (and single) meaning of this verse. When Paul spoke of "the obedience of faith" in this passage, his intent was to convey "the obedience which consists in faith." In other words, Paul's aim was to convince the Gentiles to obey the command to believe in the gospel and be saved.

---

[154] Ibid.

[155] This is known as Occam's Razor, so named for William of Occam, who posited that the solution to a given problem that assumed the fewest things was probably the correct solution. In this instance, the genitive of apposition involves the fewest assumptions, and therefore is to be preferred.

[156] Thomas, "The Principle of Single Meaning", 46

Romans 4 – The Faith of Abraham

Romans 4 is a large passage to undertake in a textual study, but it is such an important witness to the biblical definition of salvific faith that it is imperative to comment upon it here. Due to its length, only a brief survey is permissible, but that should be sufficient to see the import of the passage. It is evident from this passage that Abraham trusted that God would do what He promised, and because of this faith he was called righteous by God.

The *crux interpretum* involves keeping in view the Old Testament background surrounding this passage. First of all, the circumcision vs. uncircumcision of Abraham is a key point made by Paul. In the Old Testament, a Jew was circumcised as a sign of keeping with the covenant between God and his people (Gen 17:10, 11). Those who are not circumcised are cut off from the fellowship of faith (Gen 17:14).[157] In this

---

[157] "The meaning of "works of the law" has been a bone of contention for many years in the evangelical world. The discussion first stared in the liberal wing of Christianity but moved to the evangelical section as a response was mandated. Under the influence of Luther in his commentary on Galatians (*Luther's Works,* 26:148 ff) he contrived the idea that Paul was against works of the law and the form of Judaism that promoted a works religion/works salvation. This was followed by major works by William Sanday and Arthur C. Heedlam in their commentary *A Critical and Exegetical Commentary on the Epistle to the Romans* (ICC), (Grand Rapids, MI; Zondervan, 1957). Rudolf Bultmann carried this theme as well in his work *Primitive Christianity in its Contemporary Setting* (Thames and Hudson, 1956). This view was challenged by Jewish scholar C.G. Montefiore. He contended that Paul was only reacting against a Hellenized form of Judaism. This view was followed by G.F. Moore in *Rabbinic Theology* (1927) and W.D. Davis, *Paul and Rabbinic Judaism* (New York; Harper, 1948), p. 221ff. The issue took a turn for the modern church under the influence of E.P. Sanders and his work, *Paul and Palestinian Judaism* (Minneapolis, MN; Augsburg Fortress, 1977). This was refined and adjusted somewhat by the voluminous works of James D.G. Dunn and N.T. Wright." In this view Paul was not railing against Judaism, per se, but only a portion of teaching that was seen in the Jews who had been Hellenized in culture and theology. Hence for Paul, Jews were saved not by works of the law but by covenant ("covenantal nomism" was the phrase Sanders coined for it), and that they stayed saved and in the covenant by works. This essentially results in the assurance offered by Roman Catholic theology that states that salvation is secured as long as works continue and grace is added. In both covenantal nomism and Roman Catholicism there is no room for "presumptuous assurance". This "new perspective on Paul" as it has come to be understood by Dunn has been hotly debated and is losing its influence. See *Justification* edited by Mark Husbands and Daniel J. Treier (Downers Grove, IL; InterVarsity Press, 2004), *Justification and Variegated Nomism,* Vol. 2 edited D.A. Carson, Peter O'Brien and Mark Seifrid (Grand Rapids, MI; Baker Academic, 2004). Also see Vol. 1 of the same series and *Paul and the New Perspective: Second Thoughts on the Origins of Paul's Gospel* by Seyoon Kim (Grand Rapids, MI; Eerdmans, 2002) for a clear rebuttal of this theological issue in Pauline studies.

sense it was a work, or following a requirement. By Paul's day this had been perverted into a semi-Pelagian view of justification, where the act of circumcision *ipso facto* included a male Jew in the covenant community of Israel without any personal relationship with Yahweh or worship of Him. Paul clearly spells out in Galatians, arguably his earliest book, the true value of circumcision for justification (namely, none; 2:16; 3:6-14). It seems that Paul nuanced his argument by the time he wrote Romans to include the timing of Abraham's justification in Genesis 15:

> Is this blessing then on the circumcised, or on the uncircumcised also? For we say, "Faith was credited to Abraham as righteousness." How then was it credited? While he was circumcised, or uncircumcised? Not while circumcised, but while uncircumcised; (Rom 4:9-10)

Paul says Abraham's faith made him righteous before God while he was still uncircumcised, before he had done any kind of obedient act. It is not until after this that God enacts the covenant of circumcision in Genesis 17, and Abraham obeys. It is not until Genesis 22 that God asks for the life of Isaac, and Abraham obeys. We don't read anything of an obedient faith in Genesis 15, or here in Romans 4. In fact, the Greek form of πιστεύω in 4:3 corresponds to the LXX version of Gen 15:6. They are both aorist active indicative, and therefore there is no indication of whether or not Abraham's faith will persevere.[158] Though some commentators would point to the hiphil וְהֶאֱמִן to find a stative sense, it must be noted that the perfect form indicates a completed, rather than ongoing (or imperfect) action. The LXX translators of Genesis 15 used an aorist to translate וְהֶאֱמִן, which should give us pause when looking for any durative aspect there. Though the LXX is not considered infallible or authoritative, nevertheless it is a valuable tool for interpretation.

---

[158] Contra Piper and Fuller.

We have to look at the context of Genesis 17 and 22 for affirmation of Abraham's perseverance. The text of Genesis 15:6 tells us that Abraham was promised by God that he would be the father of a multitude of nations outnumbering the stars, and Abraham believed God. Everett Harrison makes the comment: "Abraham accepted this promise, *relying on God to fulfill it.* This was the basis on which God pronounced him righteous."[159]

The same idea continues in the New Testament. Trust in the promise of God is what justifies a person before God. Those who do good works are in right fellowship with God, those who do not are cut off *from fellowship.* The clear emphasis of Paul in Romans 4 is upon the simple trust of Abraham, as Romans 4:4-5 clearly states. To add obedience and perseverance to the semantic range of πιστεύω in Romans 4 is to shred the very fabric of Paul's argument and make his point nonsensical.[160]

---

[159] Everett F. Harrison, *Romans.* Volume 10 of *Expositors Bible Commentary* (Grand Rapids, MI; Zondervan Publishing House, 1976). 48. It seems clear that Harrison looks at reliance on the promise of God as the nature of faith, in which case it is mere trust that the facts are true, and moreover that the one who promised is speaking truth.

[160] However, the nature of faith has been mutated into a quasi-work orientation that is assumed to be included in the formal definition. John Piper often conceives that the faith that justifies is the faith that sanctifies. See John Piper, *Future Grace.* This is from the teaching of Daniel Fuller, *The Unity of the Bible,* and Norman Shepherd "The Grace of Justification" (paper dated February 8, 1979; available at http://www.hornes.org/theologia/content/norman_shepherd/the_grace_of_justification.htm) *Thirty-four Theses on Justification in Relation to Faith, Repentance, and Good Works,* presented to the Presbytery of Philadelphia of the Orthodox Presbyterian Church, November 18, 1978, Available on the Internet at: http://www.hornes.org/theologia/content/norman_shepherd/ the_34_theses.htm, 1978. Both men articulate that biblical faith must work. Fuller and Piper describe it as obedient faith or active faith. Hence if there is no work then there was no faith. Shepherd talks of justification coming about by faith and non-meritorious works. It seems that this is loading into the meaning of the word "faith" concepts that do not fit. This additional nuance of faith would then demand that all Christians must evidence "faith working through love" (Piper commenting on Paul's use of the concept in Galatians) to be Christians. This theological view of the term faith would seem to discount the variety of warnings in the NT about growing weak in faith, shipwrecked in faith or overturned in faith. These warnings seem to be addressed to Christians. Thomas Schriener deals with this issue by claiming the warnings in the NT addressed to the Christian is the way that God makes sure that Christian will respond. If they do not respond then they are in fact not Christians. See Thomas Schreiner and Ardel Caneday, *The Race Set before Us: A Biblical Theology of Perseverance & Assurance* (Downers Grove, IL; Intervarsity Press, 2001). For a clearer understanding of the nature of faith see Gordon Clark's *Faith and Saving Faith,* Larry Moyer, *Free and Clear* (Grand Rapids, MI; Kregel Publications, 1997) and Hodges, Zane, *Absolutely Free* (Dallas; Redencion Viva, 1989). Also see J.E. Botha "The Meaning of Pisteuo in the Greek New Testament", 215-228 for an evaluation of lexical dictionaries and their procedural errors involving the inclusion of

Galatians 5:6

One of the most interesting passages in the Pauline corpus utilized to provide a functional description of faith and its relationship to works is Galatians 5:6:

> [3]And I testify again to every man who receives circumcision, that he is under obligation to keep the whole Law. [4]You have been severed from Christ, you who are seeking to be justified by law; you have fallen from grace. [5] For we through the Spirit, by faith, are waiting for the hope of righteousness. [6] For in Christ Jesus neither circumcision nor uncircumcision means anything, but *faith working through love.* (italics ours)

Many from the reformed tradition understand that the only type of justifying faith is a faith that endures, and their understanding is argued from Gal 5:6 that justifying faith is "faith working through love".[161] One of the most able proponents of this view is John Piper. In his book *Future Grace*, a book that he attributes almost every page to the teaching he gained while under Dr. Daniel Fullers tutelage, he sites Galatians 5:6 fifteen times, more than any other biblical passage in his book. He states:

> My aim is to understand and explain how it is that justifying faith works through love (Galatians 5:6). My argument is that the reason justifying faith is never alone, is that it is the nature of faith to sanctify. There is something about the essence of justifying faith which makes it a morally transforming agency. Or, to put it more precisely, there is something about the faith through which pardoning grace justifies, that makes it a suitable and efficient means through which empowering grace always sanctifies. My point in this book is that the faith, which is the occasion of justification, the same faith through which sanctifying power comes to the justified sinner. There are three assumptions here. The first assumption is that justifying faith is persevering faith. Perseverance in faith is, in one sense, the condition of justification; that is, the promise of acceptance is made only to a persevering sort of faith,

theological bias in lexical studies, as discussed above. This is built from James Barr's masterful work *The Semantics of Biblical Language* (1961).

[161] See O'Brien and Seifrid, *Justification and Variegated Nomism* 2:269

and the proper evidence of it being that sort is its actual perseverance.[162]

Piper elaborates his theological perspective and its implications as he states the necessary results of a saving faith:

> ...These are just some of the conditions that the New Testament says we must meet in order to be saved in the fullest and final sense. We must believe in Jesus and receive him and turn from our sin and obey him and humble ourselves like little children and love him more than we love our family, our possessions, or our own life. This is what it means to be converted to Christ. This alone is the way of life everlasting.[163]

Piper's exegesis of Galatians 5 is presented in his most recent book, *The Future of Justification*[164] in a separate appendix that reveals the priority of this text to his theology. The book provides an excellent critique (done with an excellent irenic spirit) of N.T. Wright's version of the New Perspectives on Paul, a topic that has had many critiques and evaluations. Piper's is the most recent in a long line of presentations since the 1977 entry of E.P. Sanders seminal study concerning what he deemed "covenantal nomism." (which was called "the New Perspective on Paul by James D.G. Dunn)

Dr Piper's argument of Galatians 5:6 is a combination of possible grammatical nuance and theological assumptions concerning the lexical meaning of "faith". It receives such emphasis from Piper because, in his view, much of the divide between Protestantism and Catholicism came from the interpretation of what the phrase "faith working through love" means.[165] He goes to great lengths to discuss the inference of the middle voice to refute the Catholic idea that love is a "form" of faith due to a reflexive concept of the middle voice. He finds a close parallel in grammar with James 5:16 and

---

[162] See Piper, *Future Grace*, 26

[163] John Piper, *Desiring God* (Sisters, OR; Multnomah Publishers, 2003), 69-70

[164] John Piper, *The Future of Justification* (Wheaton, IL; Crossway Books, 2007)

[165] *The Future of Justification*, 204 This view seems close but not exact in terms of resultant theology with Paul Rainbow: *The Way, Salvation; The Role of Christian Obedience in Justification*, Chris VanLadingham: *Judgment and Justification in Early Judaism and Paul*, and Alan Stanley: *Did Jesus Teach Salvation by Works?*

then, after establishing the grammatical parallel comes to his theological conclusion:

> "A literal rendering of James 5:16 would be: "The prayer of a righteous man, becoming effective, avails much." This corresponds in Galatians 5:6 to "The faith becoming effective through love avails [justification]/" The only point I want to make is that prayer is not rain. That is, when James says that Elijah prayed and it "became effective" in drought and rain, he was not saying that prayer "expressed itself" in drought and rain. He was saying that prayer had the effect of producing drought and rain. That is analogous to how faith relates to love.
> I conclude therefore that the use of ἐνεργουμένη in the middle voice does not have the nuance implication of extending itself, with the implication that the love in which this self-extension happens is part of what faith is. That cannot be shown from the words as they are used.
> Moreover the grammar of the verse suggests that Paul is saying that justifying faith is the kind of faith that produces love. The anarthrous participle (ἐνεργουμένη) following an anarthrous noun (πίστις) is naturally construed as having an attributive relationship. That is, the natural way to read it is: "faith, which through love becomes effective." "The attributive participle stands both with and without the article and is equivalent to a relative clause."
> Therefore, even though it is possible that ἐνεργουμένη is adverbial ("faith, by means of becoming effective through love, avails justification"), this is not obvious. In fact, the effect of this unnecessary translation is to make love "the instrument of the instrument" of justification (justification is by faith love). This translation is then used as an argument that justification is not by faith alone apart from works of love, but rather that justification is by faith by means of works of love. This, I think is the opposite of what Paul teaches in Romans 3:28; 4:4-6; 5:1; 10:3-4; Philippians 3:8-9; Galatians 2:16; 3:8, 24.[166]

Piper recognizes the importance of this passage. He states:

> In one sense, the Reformation hinges on how love and faith are related in Galatians 5:6. Luther summed up the

---

[166] Ibid, 204-5

battleground this way in reference to Galatians 5:6; "This place the schoolmen do wrest unto their own opinion, whereby they teach that we are justified by charity or works. "For they say that faith, even thought it be infused from above...justifieth not, except it be formed by charity." In other words, what Luther was willing to fight over was whether ἐνεργουμένη was attributive, defining the kind of faith that justifies (his own view), or was doubly *adverbial, explaining how faith justifies* by *means* of extending itself through love. And (2) δι' ἀγάπης has an adverbial force in that it implies that the essentially justifying instrument is faith formed by love—that is, faith in the form of love.

I would argue that we stay closer to the mind of Paul by giving δι' ἀγάπης ἐνεργουμένη a simple attributive meaning. "Faith, which becomes effective through love, avails justification." The clause "which becomes effective through love: is an adjectival modifier of faith. It tells what kind of faith avails justification. Therefore, love as an expression of faith is not the instrument of justification—it does not unite us to Christ who is our perfection. Only faith does. But this faith is the kind of faith that inevitably gives rise to love."[167] (italics original)

This interpretation with its theological implications of the nature of faith is consistent with his book *Future Grace* concerning the historical creeds.[168] This view clarifies that justification is by faith alone but the faith the saves is never alone; it must be loving in action to be justifying.[169]

However, there are some questions that must be addressed before this interpretation is accepted. First, there are some who would see the use of ἐνεργουμένη as a passive and not a middle voice[170] although the middle is

---

[167] Ibid, 205-6

[168] See especially pages 21-25.

[169] This view has an interesting consequence for the doctrine of assurance. I know I am saved because I love which proves I have the type of faith that saves. Hence works are essential for proof of salvation. Hence if no works then no salvation. Therefore we can not be saved without works. Works are the means that we know we are saved. The logical circular reasoning is hard to escape.

[170] Ben Witherington III *Grace in Galatia* (Grand Rapids, MI; Eerdmans, 1998), 370

preferred by many commentators.[171] In the present tense there is no grammatical distinction between the middle and the passive, making determination of form a subjective matter. We must tread carefully when making such a large assertion over a point for which there is no objective evidence!

Second, the language used in some of Pipers evidence must not be missed. He states that "Moreover the grammar of the verse *suggests* that Paul is saying that justifying faith is the kind of faith that produces love."[172] (italics ours) Piper realizes that the grammar itself "suggests" and is not a clear or dogmatic aid to the interpretation. His conclusion is that the participle is functioning in an attributive manner and not adverbial in the clause. It is interesting that most of the grammars except for the one he cites[173] do not comment on this verse concerning the use of the participle.[174] In fact Burton believes that it is actually adverbial.

Finally, there is a lexical predisposition that assumes that faith has a more activistic nature than it actually does.[175] In order to explain the need for an attributive rather than an adverbial force, Piper appears to follow Luther as well as Calvin's formula that we are "saved by faith alone but the faith that

---

[171] F.F. Bruce *Galatians* in The New International Greek Testament Commentary (Grand Rapids; Eerdmans, 1982), 232; Ernest De Witt Burton, *A critical and exegetical commentary on the Epistle to the Galatians* The International Critical Commentary [on the Holy Scriptures of the Old and New Testaments]vol. 35 [Edinburgh; T&T Clark, 1921, 1950), 281

[172] Piper, *The Future of Justification*, 205

[173] J.H Moulton *A Grammar of the Greek New Testament* Vol 3 (Edinburgh; T.& T Clark, 1963) 3:152. However, the difficulty concerning the syntax of participles is noted by Wallace. "It is often said that mastery of the syntax of participles is mastery of Greek syntax. Why are participles so difficult to grasp? The reason is threefold: (1) *usage*–the participle can be used as a noun, adjective, adverb, or verb (and in any mood!); (2) *word order*–the participle is often thrown to the end of the sentence or elsewhere to an equally inconvenient location; and (3) *locating the main verb*–sometimes it is verses away; sometimes it is only implied; and sometimes it is not even implied! In short the participle is difficult to master because it is so versatile. But this very versatility makes it capable of a rich variety of nuances, as well as a rich variety of abuses." (*Greek Grammar*, 613)

[174] See Wallace, *Greek Grammar*; C.F.D. Moule, *An Idiom Book of New Testament Greek*; A.T. Robertson, *Grammar of the Greek New Testament in Light of Historical Research*; Max Zerwick, *Biblical Greek Illustrated by Examples* (Rome; Pontificii Instituti Biblici, 1963), and H.E. Dana and Julius R. Mantey, *A Manual Grammar of the Greek New Testament* (Toronto; Macmillan, 1957)

[175] See the above discussion on lexicography.

saves is never alone." Thus the construction must be talking about justification, and since faith always expresses itself in love that must be what Galatians 5:6 is referring to. Piper explains the nature of faith in Galatians as he states:

> Now with that understanding of faith and works let's ask why genuine faith inevitably produces love, according to Gal. 5:6. Paul isn't saying that we are justified by two things: faith and works of love. He is saying we are justified by one thing, faith, and this faith is of such a nature that it produces love like a good tree produces good fruit. Being a loving person is absolutely essential to being saved, because the faith which saves by its very essence works through love. Therefore, it is tremendously important that we see how saving faith produces love.[176]

This understanding seems similar to Luther who states:

> Faith must of course be sincere. It must be a faith that performs good works through love. If faith lacks love it is not true faith. Thus the Apostle bars the way of hypocrites to the kingdom of Christ on all sides. He declares on the one hand, "In Christ Jesus circumcision availeth nothing," i.e., works avail nothing, but faith alone, and that without any merit whatever, avails before God. On the other hand, the Apostle declares that without fruits faith serves no purpose. To think, "If faith justifies without works, let us work nothing," is to despise the grace of God. Idle faith is not justifying faith. In this terse manner Paul presents the whole life of a Christian. Inwardly it consists in faith towards God, outwardly in love towards our fellow-men.[177]

Analysis

We share with Piper a desire to distance ourselves from a Catholic understanding of justification that requires works as a means. With this common desire, there is another approach to Galatians 5 that might give a

---

[176] "SAVING FAITH PRODUCES LOVE" (Galatians 5:6-12) June 5, 1983 (Morning) Bethlehem Baptist Church.

[177] Martin Luther, *Commentary on the Epistle to the Galatians* (1535), trans. Theodore Graebner (Grand Rapids, MI; Zondervan Publishing House, 1949), Chapter 5, pp. 194-216

more contextually balanced understanding of the passage while at the same time allowing that the grammar may well be adverbial in nature.

Context:

In exegesis as in theology there needs to be a coherent, consistent, and comprehensive understanding to the text. This has been aptly articulated by E.D. Hirsh. [178] In his approach he calls for understanding the genre of a passage that entails all of the parts to govern the whole. Hence not only has Hirsh demanded that we seek for the authors intent but also that intent can only be validated as each part of the text produces a whole that can be demonstrated by the parts. Perhaps another name for this is seeking contextual comprehension that is consistent and cohesive. This means that context is king.

In the passage at hand it is critical that the context be understood. First, in the general and greater context, Paul is speaking to Christians about moving forward in their Christian life (i.e. sanctification).

- Paul is addressing this church(es) and the believers of the church reminding them that they were justified by faith and not by works of the law (2:16). In fact his concern is that having begun by the Spirit he is perplexed that they wish to continue by the law and the flesh (1:6; 3:2-3).

- Paul argues that the law is of no value to the believer since their life is to be lived in the life of Christ (2:20-21).

- The Spirit is in their hearts 4:6 and they have come to know God or be known by Him (4:9). How could they wish to go back to the law (4:9b-10)?

- The issue has to do with the fact that there are some who are trying to move the believers away from their freedom and back into the system of Mosaic Law and its entanglements that could not nor

---

[178] E.D. Hirsch Jr., *Validity in Interpretation* (Yale University; New Haven Pub 1967), 78,88, 111

cannot justify anyone; nor can it aid in sanctification (4:17; 5:7, 12).[179]

The specific context of 5:6 reveals that the audience is people who have already been set free and yet who are being tempted to go back to the law (5:1). In fact the specific aspect of the law being addressed is circumcision; if the Galatians were persuaded to submit to circumcision, they would also be required to keep the entire law (5:2-3).

It is apparent that there are some among them that are preaching such a gospel and that Paul's desire is that those opponents would mutilate themselves (utilizing an play on words and theme) (5:12). However, the believers have already been known by God and received the true gospel. They were called forth for freedom (5:1, 13), but now are in danger of consuming one another (5:15). The issue is not that they are not justified but that they need to continue in sanctification that is by the Spirit and not by the law.

The key to discerning Paul's intent in 5:6b is understanding the nature of the issue at hand. Paul's concern is that the believers who had received Christ and had been justified were seeking to be sanctified by works of the law. If they were to go back to that system as if they needed what the law could provide, it would be of no benefit to them. In fact it would be a detriment to them in that the law cannot provide for them, nor produce in them, what Paul desires or what Gods demands. If they go back to the law they are "severed" from Christ since they seek to be justified by the law. They have been cut off from Christ and "fallen" from grace (5:4).

The Arminian camp would see this as a clear proof that Christians can lose their justification.[180] The Calvinistic camp sees this as clear proof that they never had truly received justification. But the people in question had

---

[179] This is perhaps similar to the issue seen in Acts 15:5, where the argument was not over the requirements of justification but rather over the prerequisites of sanctification among non-Jewish converts.

[180] See I. Howard Marshall, *Kept by the Power of God* (Paternoster Digital; 2005), 110 and Robert Shank, *Life in the Son* (Springfield, MO; Westcott Publishers, 1960), 176, 313

received the gospel from Paul and were willing to at least go blind for him (4:12-16). In fact Paul declares of his readers that "…we through the Spirit by faith are waiting for the hope of righteousness" (5:5). Paul sees himself with his audience in that they are justified and righteous and wait for the future manifestation of hope that such a righteousness will provide- i.e., ultimate vindication and glorification of the believer in the presence of Christ.

In 5:6 Paul clarifies the inability of the law and specifically of circumcision. The law in regards to justification can accomplish nothing. It is unable. It is ἰσχύω. It does not have the power to save or to sanctify. Paul specifically ties this to the fact that "in Christ" the law is powerless. The audience and the topic have to do with Christians who have been justified. They are already "in Christ." This phrase (or an equivalent) is used no less than 11 times by Paul in Galatians,[181] and seems a shorthand way of addressing the community of the justified. In 3:12 Paul calls the Galatians "brothers", and in 3:15 he asks them where their sense of blessing has gone. This fits well with Paul's admonitions in the beginning of chapter 3 that they began their walk according to the Spirit by faith, but now were reverting to legalism for their standing with Christ and in the church. This was Paul's major concern with Peter in chapter 2.

The law will not function as an aid now that they have already come to Christ. This was clearly explained by Paul in 3:23-25 where he expounded that the law was a tutor or a guide until Christ came. These people had received Christ and so the law was not only of no benefit for justification; it was also not to be used for sanctification. They had already begun by faith in Christ in the Spirit (5:1). There was no need to go forward by law and the flesh. Paul knew they were running well but were in danger of being hindered from this truth (5:7). Therefore in 5:6 the faith in question is manifested by love.

---

[181] 1:6, 22; 2:4, 17, 20; 3:14, 22, 26, 28; 5:6, 10

Grammar

It may be as Burton comments that the participle is adverbial.[182] In fact, Piper admits that this is a grammatical possibility.[183] As Wallace[184] notes, if the participle were preceded by the article we would know that it is functioning adjectivally; even if it is anarthrous, though it may still be functioning as an attributive adjective. Wallace[185] notes that the "fourth attributive position" (i.e. no articles on either the noun or the adjective, as is the case in our passage) can be used in an attributive sense, but that is only determined by context.

If the participle is indeed adverbial, our contextual analysis above does not indicate that the Catholic view of this verse is correct. Instead, if Paul is discussing sanctification rather than justification the apparent tension in justification by grace through faith literally vanishes. The adverbial sense may indeed be accepted, because Paul is saying that the manner or means of faith is manifested by acts of love as opposed to the law. Justification is by faith not by works of the Law. Sanctification, likewise, is "by means of faith which is energized by love." The phrase can still be interpreted "Circumcision or uncircumcision means nothing [for our walk with Christ], but rather faith, becoming effective by means of love, [means everything for our walk with Christ]."[186]

However, it seems likely that Piper is correct that indeed the participle ἐνεργουμένη is acting adjectivally. In fact, it would appear rather that the entire phrase δι' ἀγάπης ἐνεργουμένη is modifying πίστις. The fact that Paul adds the modifier δι' ἀγάπης ἐνεργουμένη to πίστις tells us that indeed he is being very careful in his discussion. In no other instance of

---

[182] See Burton p. 281

[183] Piper, *The Future of Justification*, 205. The reason that he does not accept that possibility is his strong insistence that the passage is addressing justification rather than sanctification, which is addressed in the above contextual analysis.

[184] Wallace, *Greek Grammar*, 617

[185] Ibid, 310-11

[186] The quotation marks are our adaptation of Piper's interpretation of the adverbial sense (205), substituting "sanctification" for "justification."

πίστις in Galatians does Paul qualify it in any way beyond addressing its object (i.e. "faith *in Christ*")[187]; the addendum of δι' ἀγάπης ἐνεργουμένη to πίστις in this case should lead us to cautious and careful evaluation. Even if we accept Piper's analysis, though, the attributive relationship does not prove that justifying faith shows itself in love. Rather, if contextually Paul is discussing sanctification then his main point is that faith which has been energized or "becomes effective"[188] for sanctification by means of love.

In fact the forthcoming context reveals that the issue *is* sanctification, which is accomplished by the power of the Spirit as seen through love. Paul argues strongly that our walk with Christ is not by means of the flesh as motivated by law. The famous section concerning the "fruit of the Spirit" is contrasted with the works of the flesh and the manipulation of the law.

This context sheds light on the issue of 5:6. The contrast is love versus law in the life of the Christian. Paul describes the obvious conditionality and caution that walking in the Spirit was not an automatic result of the Christian life. In fact he is concerned that if they do not maintain their walk of faith, which is energized by love, they will harm each other (5:15). At the end of the chapter (an unfortunate and illogical breaking point), Paul issues a last challenge against becoming boastful, challenging one another or envying one another (5:26). In the following chapter (6:1) Paul mentions the fact that some will fail to walk in the Spirit and actually walk in the flesh, be caught in trespass and sin and be in need of restoration since they have fallen. Paul as a pastor is painfully aware that just because a caution is issued the conditionality is not hypothetical but actual.[189] Paul knew that there would

---

[187] Likewise in Romans Paul never qualifies faith. The sole exception to this is in Romans 3:28, when Paul clarifies that the faith he is discussing is "apart from works of the Law." Paul seldom qualifies the noun πίστις in his writings. Some see Romans 1:5 and 16:26 as obedience qualifying faith. It may simply be in apposition: Obedience to the gospel is faith.

[188] Piper's interpretation of the middle voice (204)

[189] Peter ended his last letter with both an appeal to faithfulness and a recognition of the danger of retrogression. (2 Peter 3:17-18)

be believers in Galatia who would continue to backslide into legalism, and Paul admonishes them to restore each other gently.

Conclusion

Faith is only known before men by deeds and actions, either by law or love. Faith before God is known intuitively and instantaneously by Him with the first initial thought. Paul instructs the Christians at Galatia, having come to Christ by faith and not by law (2:16) that they are to grow in their faith by love and not deeds of the law (2:20; 5:6, 16). Faith is indeed manifested by means of love before men. But that does not mean that the nature of faith itself results in works. The contextual clues, as well as the grammatical analysis, leads to the conclusion that Paul was not attempting in this passage to delimit the kind of faith that is effective for justification. Rather, he seeks to help the Galatians see that their standing with Christ began with faith, and in Galatians 5:6 he teaches that their sanctification continues by faith energized or "made effective" through love.

Romans 10:9-10

Many evangelistic tools (tracts, pamphlets, websites, etc.) include Romans 10:9-10 in their presentation of the good news of eternal redemption available in Christ:

> "...that if you confess with your mouth Jesus as Lord, and believe in your heart that God raised Him from the dead, you will be saved; for with the heart a person believes, resulting in righteousness, and with the mouth he confesses, resulting in salvation." (Rom 10:9-10)

Several interpretive options are popular within evangelical circles, and the one we adopt will color our view of salvation, sanctification, sin, and the entirety of the message of Scripture. We must carefully analyze the context of Romans 9-11, as well as study the important terms used in 10:9-10. The goal of this procedure is to come to an interpretation of this passage that maintains the integrity of Scripture, the freedom of the gospel of grace, and the responsibility of the believer to live under the sovereign hand of God.

The Lordship view holds that the message of Romans 10:9-10 is that a person must submit to the Lordship of Christ in order to gain eternal life. This is the view of John MacArthur.[190] In this view, Rom 10:9-10 is a concise statement of the requirements for justification and eternal life. Lordship proponents point to the confession of Jesus as κύριος as evidence that more than mere intellectual assent is in mind in these verses. Daniel Wallace points out that the construction in Greek identifies Jesus as Yahweh,[191] and Lordship proponents then further equate this confession as evidence of submission to the Lordship of Christ as the true requirement in view.[192]

Lordship proponents also argue that in light of the classical and Hellenistic usage of κύριος as implying dominion and rule, the confession of Jesus in Romans 10:9 includes a submission to His authority and dominion over a person. Emperor worship was so prevalent within the audience of the Epistle to the Romans that it is argued that the thought would naturally be transferred to the interpretation of Romans 10:9-10. No Roman would think of acknowledging the emperor as κύριος without also submitting to his authority and rule over their life.

On the other hand, if Romans 10:9-10 is a statement of the requirements of eternal life that includes more than faith, then it would seem to be in direct opposition to hundreds of New Testament verses that mandate faith alone as the requirement for eternal life (John 3:16; 20:31; Acts 16:31; Eph 2:8-9 among the many). It is also noteworthy that the argument that the concept of

---

[190] John F. MacArthur Jr., *The Gospel According to Jesus: What Does Jesus Mean When He Says, 'Follow Me'?* revised and expanded ed. (Grand Rapids: Zondervan Publishing House, 1994), 34.

[191] Daniel B. Wallace, *Greek Grammar Beyond the Basics*, 188.

[192] So John F. MacArthur, *The Gospel According to Jesus*, 28-29.

emperor worship and submission to the emperor is in mind is an example of illegitimate totality transfer.[193] To reiterate, in this error the entire semantic range of a word is brought to bear upon a single instance of that word, rather than allowing the context at hand to determine which of the many semantically possible meanings is most appropriate in a given instance. In the text at hand, there is no indication that an allusion to emperor worship is in mind, and Wallace points out that these words are not in apposition, but rather are in an object-complement construction.[194]

Other commentators on this passage hold that the message of Romans 10:9-10 is a witness of genuine evidence for the eternal state of a person. This view is very similar to (and often either interchanged or combined with) the Lordship view. Proponents of this view argue that a genuine believer in Jesus Christ will publicly confess Him. True Christians will eventually publicly identify with Christ.[195] Most commentators affirm a public confession in Romans 10:9-10.[196] This view wrestles with the face value of the statement of the text. Two conditions are in view here for salvation: belief and confession. Though the belief in verse 10 results in justification, it is the confession that leads to salvation. There is biblical evidence that our words give evidence to our inner convictions (Matt. 15:18). Jesus also declares in Matthew 10:32, "Therefore everyone who confesses Me before men, I will also confess him before My Father who is in heaven."

---

[193] See James Barr, *Semantics of Biblical Languages*, 218 for a discussion of illegitimate totality transfer, especially in TDNT.

[194] Daniel Wallace, *Greek Grammar Beyond the Basics*, 188 lists this usage's meaning as "confess that Jesus is Yahweh" rather than "confess Jesus as *kurios*/master".

[195] See John Murray, *The Epistle to the Romans*, 55–57; William B. T. Shedd, *A Critical and Doctrinal Commentary on the Epistle of St. Paul to the Romans* (Minneapolis, MN; Klock and Klock Christian Publishers, 1978), 318–19; Thomas R. Schreiner, *Romans*, Baker Exegetical Commentary on the New Testament (Grand Rapids, MI: Baker Book House, 1998), 609.

[196] So James Dunn, *Romans 9–16* in *Word Biblical Commentary Volume 38b* (Dallas; Word Books, 1988), 607; William Sanday and Arthur C. Headlam, *The Epistle to the Romans*, 290; Douglas Moo, *The Epistle to the Romans*. The New International Commentary on the New Testament (Grand Rapids, MI; Eerdmans, 1996), 657; Schreiner, *Romans,* 607; Robert Mounce, *Romans* in *New American Commentary* (Nashville, TN; Broadman and Holman, 2001), 209.

However, there are several challenges with this view. In the verses in Matthew, if Jesus is giving indications about unregenerate people becoming believers He is certainly being very vague about it. The parallel to Matthew 10:32 in Luke 12:8-9 has Christ making the confession before angels, and this makes it very unlikely that He is discussing the eternal destiny of people, in that angels have no bearing on that issue. There is also biblical evidence that there can be true believers who do not "confess" Christ, as per the discussion above regarding John 12:42. John clearly says that these people believed, and unless believers can go to eternal damnation confession is not best seen as salvific. The argument that these people eventually confessed Christ is an argument from silence, as is the argument that their belief was "false faith."

Still other commentators take a synonymous view. This view holds that the two terms in Romans 10:9-10 are synonymous: believing in the heart *is* confessing Jesus as Lord. Some Free Grace advocates take this position.[197] This view sees parallelism in Romans 10:9-10. The statements "believe in your heart" and "confess with your mouth" may be taken as parallel statements. Some also see a parallel with the confession of 1 John 1:9, and equate this as a private confession to God and not before men.

However, it seems that the statements of Romans 10:9-10 are chiastic and not parallel. They are arranged in this manner:

(A)   that if you confess with your mouth Jesus as Lord

    (B)   and believe in your heart that God raised Him from the dead you will be saved

    (B')   for with the heart a person believes resulting in righteousness

(A')   and with the mouth he confesses resulting in salvation

---

[197] Livingston Blauvelt Jr., "Does the Bible Teach Lordship Salvation?" *Bibliotheca Sacra,* 143 (Jan 1986): 39–41; Charles C. Ryrie, *So Great Salvation* (Wheaton, IL: Victor Books, 1989), 70–73; Everett F. Harrison, "Matthew," *Expositor's Bible Commentary*, ed. Frank E. Gaebelein (Grand Rapids, MI: Zondervan Publishing House, 1995), 112; J. Ronald Blue, "Go, Missions," *Bibliotheca Sacra* 141 (October-December 1984): 347-49.

With this in mind, the confession of verse 9 is best paralleled with the confession of verse 10, and not with the belief of verse 9. Unless we blur the distinctions between words (which is exegetically unwise), Paul has been careful to separate the heart and the mouth. Belief does not take place in the mouth, nor does confession take place in the heart. These distinctions are not best minimized. Confession (ὁμολογέω) is normally used in a public sense.[198] Though exceptions exist (1 John 1:9 appears to be one), there is nothing in context here to suggest that a private confession is in mind.

All of the above interpretations contain serious questions and concerns regarding their validity. Perhaps a reevaluation of these verses will assist us in gaining understanding of Paul's message in this often-used passage. By looking at the context of Paul's argument, as well as his use of terms in Romans, we can gain insight into Paul's intent for Romans 10:9-10.

Reevaluation of two key terms in Romans will assist in understanding the interpretation of the passage in question. Especially in passages as well-known as this it is common to bring presupposed meaning into terms used in a particular way in a particular context. However, proper hermeneutics demands that interpreters avoid this pitfall.

1. Justification: This term (δικαιοσύνη) is undeniably Paul's favorite term for redemption. It is beyond argument that in Pauline usage this is a legal term referring to the imputation of divine righteousness that a person receives at the moment of saving faith. Romans 3:21-5:8 discusses justification in great detail, culminating in the great blessing available to believers in 5:9-11. In this section, Paul's *magnum opus* on justification, no mention is made of "confessing Jesus as Lord" in order to receive the justification under discussion. Paul stresses again and

---

[198] See J.P. Louw, & E.A. Nida *Greek-English lexicon of the New Testament : Based on semantic domains* (New York: United Bible Societies; 1996) 33.221, 33.274, 33.275. See also BDAG s.v. ὁμολογέω

again the need for faith alone as the requirement for justification in these chapters, and it seems odd that Paul would add the need for confession or submission at the late point of chapter 10. In Romans, nothing more is needed to have eternal life than to be justified in the sight of God (3:20; 4:2-5). This is in perfect harmony with the statements of 10:10 concerning justification: when a person *believes*, they are *justified*. Salvation/save/saved: A study of these terms (σῴζω and σωτηρία) shows that Paul does not necessarily equate salvation and justification. Romans 13:11 tells us, "…for now salvation is nearer to us than when we believed." Paul can speak of justified people who are not yet "saved," proving that at least in this instance Paul does not necessarily equate salvation and justification. Paul is certainly capable of using the term "salvation" to refer to what we normally call glorification. We must in this instance resist the modern evangelical usage of "saved" and "salvation" and attempt to analyze the Pauline usage of this key word group.

With that in mind, we must look at Paul's usage of "salvation" and "saved" in Romans to understand his usage of it in 10:9-10. Only by careful observation of each usage can we discern his semantic understanding.

> 1:16: This first usage in Romans is within the first thematic statement of the letter.[199] Paul says that the "good news" is deliverance/salvation to the believing ones. This salvation is juxtaposed with the wrath of God in 1:18, and therefore it is appropriate to view this deliverance as removal from the wrath of God in v.18. Upon closer inspection of v. 18, it becomes clear that deliverance from eternal damnation is not in view in this verse. Paul uses the present tense, "The wrath of God is being revealed" (NIV) as a present statement of fact, not an eschatological

---

[199] James D.G. Dunn, *Romans 1–8,* Word Biblical Commentary (Dallas: Word Books, 1988), 38a: 36, 46

judgment. Three times Paul discusses the result of His wrath: allowing those under wrath to delve deeper and deeper into sin.

5:9-11: Paul has avoided using the words "save" or "salvation" in his discussion of justification by faith (3:21-4:25), and this is the next place where it surfaces.[200] Paul states the message clearly here:

> Much more then, having now **been justified** by His blood, we **shall be saved from the wrath of God** through Him. For if while we were enemies we were reconciled to God through the death of His Son, much more, **having been reconciled, we shall be saved** by His life. And not only this, but we also exult in God through our Lord Jesus Christ, through whom we have now received the reconciliation. (NASB, emphasis mine)

Though justification has taken place in the past, salvation is seen in the future. Paul also explicitly mentions that the salvation in view is salvation from "the wrath of God," which links this verse with 1:16-18.[201] This connection leads to the conclusion that the salvation in mind is deliverance from the current, earthly displeasure and discipline of God, as it does in 1:18. Eschatology is not in view here.

8:24: The next use of "saved" comes in the context of not being slaves to sin (6:6), and the problem of our mortal body. This is the only aorist tense occurrence of "saved" in Romans, but when linked with the prepositional phrase "in this hope" it throws the thought back into the future. We can be "delivered" from bondage to sin,

---

[200] John F. Hart, "Why Confess Christ? The Use and Abuse of Romans 10:9-10." In *Journal of the Grace Evangelical Society Volume 12:2* (Autumn 1999), 17.

[201] See Rene Lopez, *Romans Unlocked* (Springfield, MO; 21st Century Press, 2005), 108-111 for a discussion on the article of previous reference and the connection of "wrath" in 5:9 Wesly L. Uplinger, "The Problem of Confession in Romans 10:9-10." Th.M. Thesis, Dallas Theological Seminary, 1968

and in fact that is our calling. There is no contextual need to see this usage as referring to justification.

Chapters 9-11: This unit comprises a discussion on the past, present, and future relationship of the Lord and Israel. The final occurrences of "save" in Romans are here. In 9:27 Paul quotes Isaiah 10:22, where the clear connotation is deliverance from enemies (the LXX uses σώζω to translate the Hebrew שׁוּב [shub], translated "return"). 11:26 is also contained in a quote which clearly deals with deliverance from oppression (Isa 59:20). In the Millennial Kingdom, Israel will indeed be delivered from oppression and bondage to other nations.

Analysis of the words of Romans 10:9-10, then, gives us an understanding of Paul's intent. Paul's use of justification and salvation throughout Romans is consistent; justification results from imputed righteousness received by faith, and salvation or being "saved" refers, in Romans, to the deliverance of a believer from the current displeasure and "wrath" of God in time. This leads to an interpretation of Romans 10:9-10 that meshes with Pauline usage of terms in Romans, as well as fitting the overall context of chapters 9-11.[202]

In this view, described as the "deliverance" view, when a person believes and calls upon divine help, God can and will deliver that person from oppression or discipline. Seen this way, verses 9-10 reiterate the truths Paul quoted from Deuteronomy 30:12-14 in verse 8. Again, the text says,

> ...that if you confess with your mouth Jesus as Lord,
> and believe in your heart that God raised Him from the
> dead, you will be saved; for with the heart a person
> believes, resulting in righteousness, and with the mouth he
> confesses, resulting in salvation.

---

[202] For further insight and discussion, see Rene Lopez, *Romans Unlocked*, 187-239. This line of reasoning comes from Zane Hodges *Is Salvation Really Free* (unpublished document). Some of this thinking is also articulated in *A Commentary on Romans* by Andres Nygren.

When one believes, they receive God's imputed righteousness, the same term Paul uses elsewhere in Romans to refer to justification by faith (1:17; 3:21-4:25; 10:6). At this point in Pauline soteriology, the person in view is regenerate, justified, and has eternal standing before God. Further, when that believer confesses or calls upon Yahweh, they will be "saved." From the immediate context as well as a study of Paul's usage of the term, it is clear that "saved" refers to divine deliverance from temporal wrath. The wrath, as 1:18 and 5:9-10 make clear, is currently being poured out against all ungodliness and sin. This is the "salvation" that is in view in Romans 10:10. The Old Testament backdrop to the term "saved" is only strengthened by Paul's liberal use of LXX quotations in this section on the fate of Israel.

Paul reinforces this truth by quoting Isaiah 28:16 in verse 11 to console those who believe and confess (or call for divine aid). The passage in Isaiah was written at a time when Israel was calling on pagan gods for assistance, so Paul uses Isaiah's words to encourage believers to rely on Yahweh for help. Paul may be drawing an analogy between the Assyrian invasion of Isaiah and the coming destruction of Jerusalem in A.D. 70. The pivotal discussion of Romans 9-11 deals primarily with Israel.

However, Paul also shows here that the principles for Christian deliverance apply to Jews and Greeks alike. Joel's admonition that "whoever will call on the name of the Lord will be saved" gives further evidence for the deliverance from wrath view. Calling on the name of the Lord is a practice for believers only (see Gen 26:25; 1 Kings 18:24-27; Acts 7:59; 1 Cor 1:2). The phrase identifies believers who publicly invoked the aid of God by calling on His name (Acts 9:14). In Joel 2:32, calling on the name of the Lord explicitly removes the believer from the experience of God's wrath as it is poured out on others.

Verses 14-17 show the progression (in reverse order) for Christian deliverance. To be "saved" one must call on the name of the Lord, and Paul gives us the order of events in 14-15:

   a.   First, the preacher must be sent to them.
   b.   Then, the preacher must preach the message to them.
   c.   They must next hear the preacher and believe his message, becoming regenerate in the process.
   d.   Lastly they must call on God for deliverance from their current discipline.

Verses 16-17 tell us that Paul did indeed have Israel primarily in mind for this deliverance. By quoting Isaiah, he reminds us that most of Israel rejected the "word of Christ" and in so doing prevented their own deliverance.

It is clear now that the "Romans Road" is a sincere, yet misguided evangelistic tool. Romans 10:9-10 teach us about the justice of God in disciplining Israel at the present time, and also apply to Jew or Gentile in being delivered from divine discipline. As believers, our responsibility when being chastised is to call on the name of the Lord (i.e. confess and repent) to allow God to remove our discipline and restore us.

Romans 10:9-10 cannot be shown to support the supposition that a person must submit to the Lordship of Jesus to be delivered from eternal damnation, because it does not intend to say anything about what we typically refer to as "salvation." Instead, it points the way for Israel to be returned to their place of blessing and special favor, and (as Paul reminds us in 10:12) also speaks to those of us who are Gentiles. Romans 10:9-10 deal with sanctification, and that is how we must use them in our ministry.[203]

---

[203] Much of the preceding insights come from an unpublished commentary on the book of Romans dictated by Zane Hodges (n.d.) Mr. Hodges is presently working on a full commentary on the book of Romans for future publication. Many of his thoughts have been incorporated by some of the footnoted authors in this paper.

Ephesians 2:8-9

This passage is extremely important for this study because it is used by Lordship advocates to support the doctrine of irresistible grace and perseverance of the saints. They reason that since faith is here shown to be a gift from God, the faith that He gives must necessarily bring with it a change in life.[204] The question is whether faith in this passage is the gift of God, as Calvin claimed. It is acknowledged that some modern scholars have abandoned Calvin's premise for this passage, but some still hold that this passage teaches that faith is a direct gift of God[205], and therefore we must consider the merit of this position. The text reads:

"**τῇ γὰρ χάριτί** ἐστε **σεσῳσμένοι διὰ πίστεως**·
καὶ **τοῦτο** οὐκ ἐξ ὑμῶν, θεοῦ τὸ δῶρον· οὐκ ἐξ ἔργων,
ἵνα μή τις καυχήσηται." (Ephesians 2:8-9)

Verse eight is the center of the argument. We must notice the structure of the verse. The phrase τῇ γὰρ χάριτί has been placed in emphatic first position. It is also notable that the verb is a perfect passive participle in the nominative case combined with a present tense of εἰμί, forming a perfect periphrastic.[206] The perfect usually indicates an event in past time with results that spill into the present time. Gregory Sapaugh explains the force of the periphrastic:

> Salvation is expressed by the periphrastic participle este sesōsmenoi ("you have been saved"). The perfect tense of the participle signifies the present state resulting from a prior occurrence. In other words, the Ephesian believers are now saved due to their past faith. However, the time element is not so clear and the focus may simply be on the present state of salvation with no implication of the prior action which produced it.[207]

---

[204] The divine antecedent to the divine gift of faith is divine election and calling, both of which are irresistible in this line of reasoning.

[205] See William B.T. Shedd, *Dogmatic Theology*, (Phillipsburg, NJ; P&R Publishing, 2005 2:472; Louis Berkhof, *Systematic Theology*, 503

[206] Daniel Wallace, *Greek Grammar*, 648

[207] Gregory P. Sapaugh, "Is Faith a Gift? A Study of Ephesians 2:8" in *Journal of the Grace Evangelical Society 7:1* (Spring 1994), 35. Also see the excellent and seminal work by Timothy

The periphrastic gives this participle the force of a declined verb, as opposed to the discussion above regarding substantival participles. Sapaugh's analysis of the *Aktionsart* of this occurrence, though, is useful; though the perfect indicates past-time completed action, the focus is on the results that spill into the present.[208]

Normally this verse translated by Lordship advocates, "For by grace you have been saved, through faith, and this [faith] is not of yourselves, it is the gift of God." The Lordship view is valid in translation *if* the antecedent of the demonstrative pronoun is πίστεως, but this is not the case. Grammatically, τοῦτο is a neuter singular nominative. Χάριτί is a feminine singular dative, and πίστεως is a feminine singular genitive. The demonstrative pronoun normally must agree with its antecedent in both gender and number,[209] and therefore neither πίστεως nor χάριτί can be rightly seen as the antecedent of τοῦτο.

The demonstrative is in the same case as the participle, and nominatives usually cohere. Also the phrase "by grace you have been saved" is first used in verse five, which sets the tone of the passage. Faith is not in view here, but instead the entire experience of salvation is in view. It actually makes textual and contextual sense to say that the demonstrative is specifically tied

---

R. Nichols, "Reverse-Engineered Outlining: A Method for Epistolary Exegesis." CTS Journal 7 (April – June 2001), pp. 16-58.

[208] Daniel Wallace, *Greek Grammar*, 573, states concerning the emphasis of the perfect tense:
> The force of the perfect tense is simply that it describes an event that, completed in the past (we are speaking of the perfect indicative here), has results existing in the present time (i.e., in relation to the time of the speaker). Or, as Zerwick puts it, the perfect tense is used for "indicating not the past action as such but the present 'state of affairs' resulting from the past action."

[209] The demonstrative pronoun *may* occasionally agree with its antecedent *ad sensum*, i.e. in sense and not grammatically. In these instances the antecedents involve "natural agreement," meaning the demonstrative and its antecedent naturally adhere. Instances of the *constructio ad sensum* are rare. See Daniel Wallace, *Greek Grammar*, 330-332. It is certainly worth noting that Wallace does not list this verse in any of his examples for the *constructio ad sensum*, even the debatable examples.

to the periphrastic, and on a broader scale, it is tied to the whole participial phrase. As Sapaugh concisely summarizes:

> A neuter pronoun may also be used to refer to a phrase or summarize a thought. This seems to be the best solution in Ephesians 2:8. Touto refers back to the entire phrase tē gar chariti este sesōsmenoi dia tēs pisteōs ("for by grace you have been saved through faith"). Therefore, the whole salvation experience, which occurs by means of the grace of God when a person believes, is what is referred to by kai touto ouk ex hymōn ("and this not of yourselves").
>
> This position is further supported by the parallelism between ouk ex hymōn ("and this not of yourselves") in 2:8 and ouk ex ergōn ("not of works") in 2:9. The latter phrase would not be meaningful if it referred to pisteōs ("faith"). Instead, it clearly means that salvation is "not of works." Therefore, these two clauses refer back to the introductory clause of 2:8 and the entire salvation experience.[210]

The following is one way to diagram this passage based on this textual arrangement. This seems to be the most natural interpretation for the flow of the passage, and thus throughout the entire process, salvation is the gift of God by grace through faith. As the diagram below shows, salvation is the antecedent to τοῦτο.

---

[210] Gregory C. Sapaugh, "Is Faith a Gift?", 39-40

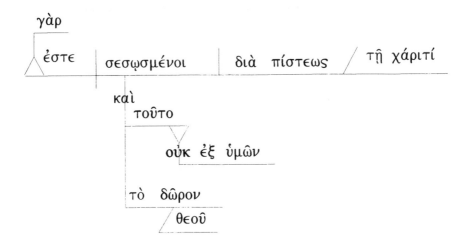

In terms of the interpretation of the passage it is worth noting that Paul's great emphasis in this verse is the clause Τῇ γὰρ χάριτί, which is placed in emphatic position[211] by virtue of being thrown to the front of the sentence. What then is the gift? Again, Sapaugh provides excellent insight:

> Since touto refers to the previous phrase tē gar chariti este sesōsmenoi dia tēs pisteōs ("for by grace you have been saved through faith"), Theou to dōron ("the gift of God") is salvation. God gives everlasting life, by grace, to the one who believes in Christ. Theou ("of God") is placed first here for emphasis and to create a contrast with ouk ex hymōn ("not of yourselves"). Grace is not a gift, it is the *basis* of the gift. Faith is not a gift, it is the means by which the gift is received. Salvation is the gift.

Roy Aldrich speaks to the heart of the issue:

> In the Bible there is no clear and dogmatic statement that saving faith is a gift of God. On the other hand, the Bible clearly states the way in which faith is obtained: "Faith cometh by hearing, and hearing by the word of God" (Rom 10:17). The Scriptures speak of saving faith as "thy faith" (Luke 7:50), "his faith" (Rom 4:5), and "their faith" (Matt 9:2) ; but never as the faith of God."

---

[211] See Gregory C Sapaugh, "Is Faith a Gift?", 34

It can be agreed that saving faith is the gift of God in
the broad sense in which all things come from God (1 Cor
4:7; Rom 11:35, 36). However, this is entirely different
from the position that an unsaved person cannot believe
until he first receives a special gift of faith from God. Such
a doctrine is opposed by the "whosover" passages of the
Bible, and by passages which beseech the sinner to be
saved (i.e., John 3:16; 2 Cor 5:20).[212]

Indeed, Ephesians 2:8-9 is a beautiful and theologically critical discussion

of soteriology, and as such is central to evangelical theology. With a verse

as important as this it becomes especially vital to stay within the boundaries

of the text and not misuse it out of zeal. Paul does not teach that faith is a

gift of God in this passage; he teaches that all of salvation is a gift. We must

not ask the text to say something the author does not intend to say; otherwise

our hold on the authority and inerrancy of Scripture slips away and we use

texts for our own agenda.

Miscellaneous Pauline Texts

The classic case of the jailer of Philippi in Acts 16 is a strong one. Paul

and Silas tell the jailer "πίστευσον ἐπὶ τὸν κύριον Ἰησοῦν καὶ σωθήσῃ."

This is an aorist active imperative with ἐπὶ, and there is no explicit or

implicit reference to obedience here. Simply believe and you will be saved.

Though undoubtedly Paul and Silas had more things to say to the Philippian

jailer, Luke only records for us the pertinent facts: when asked the

requirements for eternal life, Paul tells him to believe in the aorist tense. The

above discussion on the semantic range of πιστεύω leads here to a view of

the gospel that is striking in its simplicity.

In Romans 14:1 Paul says that those who are "weak in faith" should be

welcomed. The passage is specifically dealing with lifestyle issues and the

Christian walk, which leads to the interpretation that it is possible to have

---

[212]Roy Aldrich, "The Gift of God" in *Bibliotheca Sacra Volume 122*, (July 1965), 252.

true faith, and yet for that faith to be weak. In 1 Thessalonians 3:10 Paul says that he hopes to see them in person to "καταρτίσαι τὰ ὑστερήματα τῆς πίστεως ὑμῶν," which is literally translated "to supply what is deficient in your faith." Even stronger, Paul could be referring to a "defective" faith in this passage. Apparently someone can have a defective faith, but we must remain aware that there are no contextual clues here to indicate that Paul is doing anything other than encouraging believers in Christ. This is not a statement of the possibility of spurious faith; it is an encouragement from Paul to the Thessalonian believers that he longs to see them and help them mature.

In 1 Timothy 1:18-19 Paul is encouraging Timothy, based on prophecies made concerning him, to hold on to his faith and good conscience. Following this, Paul makes an amazing statement. "ἥν τινες ἀπωσάμενοι περὶ τὴν πίστιν ἐναυάγησαν, ὧν ἐστιν Ὑμέναιος καὶ Ἀλέξανδρος, οὓς παρέδωκα τῷ σατανᾷ, ἵνα παιδευθῶσιν μὴ βλασφημεῖν." (1 Timothy 1:19-20) This is literally translated, "Which some, by rejecting this, have shipwrecked concerning their faith," and Paul goes on to name Hymenaeus and Alexander as examples. He even goes so far as to say that he has given them over to Satan in order to teach them a lesson. I Corinthians 5:5 makes a similar statement regarding handing someone over to Satan.[213]

We must take careful consideration of context and observe the text carefully to make correct interpretation regarding the eternal state of these people.[214] It is important to note here that Paul uses the term shipwrecked.

---

[213] The passage in I Corinthians deals with a member of the church living in incest, and the instruction Paul gives them is to deliver that person to Satan to destroy him physically, so that his soul might be saved. See the discussion in the section on James 2 regarding the salvation of the soul.

[214] Paul in 1 Tim 4:16, realizes that even the concept of salvation could be polymorphous and in a sense contingent. "Pay close attention to yourself and to your teaching; persevere in these things, for as you do this you will ensure salvation both for yourself and for those who hear you." Eternal life is not contingent once received. But Paul does state that he and Timothy need to pay attention to their teaching, and they will ensure salvation for themselves and for those whom they teach in proportion to their attendance to their lives and teaching. Clearly the context

The idea is that their ship was sailing smooth for awhile, but it encountered rough seas and floundered. It is no small point to observe that the fact that they shipwrecked their faith means that they must first have a faith to shipwreck. As Wilkin puts it, "One can only experience shipwreck if he was at one time on board."[215] So assuming Hymenaeus and Alexander had faith (which is the natural assumption of their association with the ones whose faith was shipwrecked), and it is also assumed that their faith is in Christ, we can logically deduce that believers can experience shipwreck. It seems evident that Paul wanted them to get back on track, but he nevertheless held out the real possibility that a believer could fail to persevere and suffer "shipwreck" with respect to his faith. This is especially the case when it seems rather extreme to give an unbeliever over to Satan, but since Satan can do nothing eternally to a Christian, it makes sense to use him to teach a lesson.

Luke 22:32[216] is another verse that is rather perplexing if one takes the view that faith is a gift of God, for then God's gift is imperfect. Here, Jesus allows for the possibility that faith can fail. The text reads "ἐγὼ δὲ ἐδεήθην περὶ σοῦ ἵνα μὴ ἐκλίπῃ ἡ πίστις σου" ("but I have prayed for you, that your faith may not fail"). The word translated fail here (ἐκλίπῃ) carries the connotation "to give out"[217] and also "to cease, to stop, to forsake"[218]. The verb ἐκλείπω is only found four times in the New Testament, with three of those occurrences coming from Luke (Luke 16:9; 22:32; 23:45; Hebrews 1:12).

---

has to do with the issue of false teaching. If Timothy will pay attention to his life and teaching then he can be assured that he and those who hear him will be delivered from the false doctrine in a sense similar to Philippians 3.

[215] Robert Wilkin, "Repentance and Salvation Part 5: New Testament Repentance: Repentance in the Epistles and Revelation" in *Journal of the Grace Evangelical Society 3:2* (Autumn 1990), 28

[216] This verse is not Pauline, but since Luke was such a close associate of Paul, and clearly associated with him theologically, it is not a stretch to include Lukan material in our discussion of Pauline texts.

[217] Louw-Nida *Greek-English Lexicon*, 57.46

[218] Ibid, 68.36

This verse further militates against the position that faith is an immediate gift of God; otherwise God's gift is unreliable and suspect. Though it may be possible to hold that Jesus has guaranteed Peter's faithfulness and therefore God's gift of faith is indeed reliable, it nevertheless stands that without the intercessory prayer of Jesus Peter stood in the stark possibility of his faith failing him. In light of this, it seems best to view faith as a mediate activity of man rather than an immediate gift of God, especially in light of the analysis of Ephesians 2 above. The gift is irrevocable and indefectible but the faith that appropriates it is defectible. Robert Preus[219] reminds us that for Luther faith was pure passivity and receptivity.

Hebrews 10:38-39

The authorship of the book of Hebrews is a debated topic, and not easily solved. Some believe that Paul wrote Hebrews; many hold that the author of Hebrews will forever stand unknown as a testimony to the power of the message over the messenger. The discussion of Hebrews 10:38-39 is placed within the discussion of the Pauline material because some would view it as belonging there. Neither of the authors believes Hebrews was written by Paul, but the discussion is included here for lack of a more appropriate position.

These verses provide the introduction for one of the most famous passages in all of Scripture: the "Hall of Faith" of Hebrews 11. The author of Hebrews introduces the verses in question by reminding his audience that they need endurance, and also gives them a reason for persevering:

> Therefore, do not throw away your confidence, which has a great reward. For you have need of endurance, so that when you have done the will of God, you may receive what was promised. For yet in a very little while, He who is coming will come, and will not delay. (Heb 10:35-37)

---

[219] See Preus, "The Perennial Problem of the Doctrine of Justification."

After this rousing introduction the author gives a stern reminder of the other side of the coin:

"ὁ δὲ δίκαιός μου ἐκ πίστεως ζήσεται, **καὶ ἐὰν ὑποστείληται**, οὐκ εὐδοκεῖ ἡ ψυχή μου ἐν αὐτῷ. ἡμεῖς δὲ οὐκ ἐσμὲν ὑποστολῆς εἰς ἀπώλειαν ἀλλὰ πίστεως εἰς περιποίησιν ψυχῆς." (Hebrews 10:38-39)

> "But My righteous one shall live by faith; And if he shrinks back, My soul has no pleasure in him. But we are not of those who shrink back to destruction, but of those who have faith to the preserving of the soul.

Notice the conditional clause "And if he shrinks back, my soul has no pleasure in him." It would appear that the possibility exists that a "righteous one" may reach a point in their life where their faith may fail. If this happens, God says He will have no pleasure in this person. What happens to the person that shrinks back? They face the possibility of ἀπώλειαν/destruction. This probably refers to physical death.[220] The next verse says "we are not of those who shrink back into destruction, but [we are those] of faith unto the preserving/saving of the soul." This is where great contention lies in the debate.[221] Most regard the *preservation of soul* to mean eternal salvation. However, this can mean preserving physical life. Joseph Dillow comments:

> In order to avoid the possibility of this sin to physical death, this discipline resulting in ruin of one's physical life, we must persevere in faith. The danger is that they will not. And if that occurs, that is, if "he shrinks back," then God will have no pleasure in him. This is simply an understatement (litotes) for "God will be very angry with the Christian who behaves in this way.[222]

---

[220] Refer to Joseph C. Dillow, *The Reign of the Servant Kings* (Hayesville, NC; Schoettle Publishing Co., 1993), 111-133 for a discussion of the temporal nature of this destruction.

[221] For an evaluation and exposition of the entire section see my Fred Chay, *A Strategy of Spiritual Motivation in the Book of Hebrews* (D. Min. diss.; Dallas Theological Seminary, 1990).

[222] Jospeh C. Dillow, *Reign of the Servant Kings*, 337

It is evident then that a person who has true faith can indeed shrink back from that faith, and lose the favor of God upon his life. This is not best viewed as eternal favor, but temporal favor and blessing in time.[223]

Synthesis of Pauline Texts

After carefully reviewing the Pauline corpus, we can see that his unified message is consistent with his startling statement in Romans 4:5, "But to the one who does not work, but believes in Him who justifies the ungodly, his faith is credited as righteousness." An analysis of the Pauline corpus has shown that texts frequently cited as lynchpin arguments in support of ongoing commitment and obedience have been misappropriated for that use. Paul clearly maintained the distinction of the freeness of the gospel of faith alone in Christ alone, with no works being added either in the initial act of justification or as a condition of verification or evidence of justification. The discussion in Romans 10:9-10 shows us that for Paul, sanctification and obedience to the Lord were vital concepts that demand our attention as disciples of Jesus Christ. Just as firmly, though, our analysis has shown that this discussion, for Paul, has no bearing whatsoever on soteriology.

The Perennial Problem of James 2

James 2:14-26

Finally we come to the chief text in the debate over the nature of saving faith. Both sides of the Lordship debate utilize James 2:14-26 in their discussion over the nature of the faith that delivers a person from eternal condemnation. As such it demands our attention. To get to the heart of James' message we must, as with every text we have studied, attempt to remove as much theological presupposition and preunderstanding as possible

---

[223] For an exhaustive treatment of the concept of "Saving the Soul" seen in the synoptic Gospels, see Fred Chay, *A Textual and Theological Exposition of the Logion: The Salvation of the Soul*, (Ph.D. diss; Trinity Theological Seminary, 2003)

and carefully analyze this contentious pericope. This text is the crown jewel in the discussion of saving faith, and we must allow James to speak to us and guide us in our analysis of this critical concept.

This passage has come under great dispute, and not only recently. Martin Luther based his theory of contradiction between Paul and James to a great extent on this passage. The fact that Luther placed James in the appendix of his New Testament bears witness to the fact that this is passage has caused many a careful scholar great pain.

The dilemma here is partly based on dialogue structure. James is having a discussion with a hypothetical accuser, and the problem arises when trying to figure out where the accuser's dialogue ends and James' begins. The most widely held view is that the accuser stops at the end of verse 18; others carry the accuser through verse 19.

In either case the predominant interpretation is that true faith works. In verse 14, the text says, "Τί τὸ ὄφελος, ἀδελφοί μου, ἐὰν πίστιν λέγῃ τις ἔχειν ἔργα δὲ μὴ ἔχῃ; μὴ δύναται ἡ πίστις σῶσαι αὐτόν;" ("What use is it, my brethren, if someone says he has faith but he has no works? Can that faith save him?"). The argument says that only working faith saves. John MacArthur summarizes the message well:

> James sounds almost as if he were writing to twentieth-century "no-lordship" advocates. He says that people can be deluded into thinking they believe when in fact they do not, and he says that the single factor that distinguishes counterfeit faith from the real thing is the righteous behavior inevitably produced in those who have authentic faith.
>
> These are the questions the "lordship salvation" debate must ultimately answer: Is it enough to know and understand and assent to the facts of the gospel—even holding the "inward conviction" that these truths apply to me personally—and yet never shun sin or submit to the Lord Jesus? Is a person who holds that kind of belief guaranteed eternal life? Does such a hope constitute faith in the sense in which Scripture uses the term?

James expressly teaches that it does not. Real faith, he
says, will produce righteous behavior. And the true
character of saving faith may be examined in light of the
believer's works.[224]

He bases his analysis of the passage on several factors. First, he notes
that even though James repeatedly writes to his "brothers," this does not
prove that they were regenerate. He says, "James surely knew that it would
be read by all who identified with the churches, and thus the warnings to
false professors are both essential and appropriate."[225] Joseph Pak agrees
with MacArthur in his Ph.D. dissertation:

The fact that James is writing to Jewish believers
renders weak the argument that since James addresses
them as brothers the readers must have been all genuine
believers. There are many examples in which Jews (not
Jewish believers but Jews in general) are addressed or
referred to as brothers in the New Testament (e.g., Acts
2:29, 37; 3:17, 22; 7:2, 23, 25, 26, 37; 13:26, 38; 22:1;
23:1, 5, 6; 28:17, 21; Heb 7:5). These references make it
clear that "brethren" was a common way in which the Jews
addressed one another. So when a Jewish Christian
community is addressed (as is the case with James' letter),
addressing the readers as "brothers" does not necessarily
indicate that the writer views all the readers as genuine
believers.[226]

Further, MacArthur declares that the reference to "save" in 2:14-26 "must
carry the full soteriological significance (v.1). James is speaking of eternal
salvation."[227]

MacArthur explains that the guiding interpretation of the phrase
"salvation of the soul" in 1:21 (which then guides the interpretation of the
2:14-26 pericope) is found in Matthew 10:28, There Jesus said, "Do not fear

---

[224]John F. MacArthur, "Faith According to the Apostle James" in *Journal of the Evangelical
Theological Society Volume 33* (March 1990), 16-17
[225] Ibid, 29
[226] Joseph K. Pak, "A Study of Selected Passages on Distinguishing Marks of Genuine and False
Believers" (Ph.D. diss., Dallas Theological Seminary, 2001), 223
[227] John F. MacArthur, "Faith According to the Apostle James", 24

those who kill the body but are unable to kill the soul; but rather fear Him who is able to destroy both soul and body in hell."

The Lordship position, then, is that the message of James 2:14-26 clearly teaches that a person can ascertain the validity of their standing with respect to eternal life by way of examining their righteous behavior. This passage is used to support the Reformed maxim, "Faith alone saves, but the faith that saves is never alone." MacArthur chides his opponents in the conclusion of his article on this passage:

> Defenders of "no-lordship salvation" lean too heavily on the assumptions of a predetermined theological system. They often draw their support from presupposed dispensationalist distinctions (salvation/discipleship, carnal/spiritual believers, gospel of the kingdom/gospel of grace, faith/repentance). They depend too much on hypothetical paradigms and illustrations versus didactic material. They frequently employ logical rather than Biblical arguments. Curiously, they may acknowledge the truth of a passage like James 2 and yet fail to follow through with its implications in their systematic soteriology.[228]

To determine the validity of Dr. MacArthur's analysis, we must turn to the text itself and allow exegesis and proper hermeneutical approach to guide our discussion. We must, in other words, heed Dr. MacArthur's admonition in the closing of his paper:

> A reminder of this simple axiom is in order: Our theology must be Biblical before it can be systematic. We must start with Scripture and build our theology from there, not read into God's Word unwarranted presuppositions. Scripture is the only appropriate gauge by which we may ultimately measure the correctness of our doctrine.[229]

---

[228]Ibid, 33.
[229]Ibid.

Excursus 1: The Practical Syllogism

At this point in our discussion it is important to look at the logical implications of the Reformed maxim, "Faith alone saves, but the faith that saves is never alone." Reformed scholars will argue that it is faith alone which saves a person, and that God looks at only a person's faith and not their works in determining their eternal destiny. However, they argue from texts such as the one under consideration that a true, salvific faith will necessarily and inevitably lead to a life of good works.

If this maxim were broken down to its simplest logical terms, it could be summarized, "If faith, then works." What remains to be seen is whether the syllogism can function logically. In other words, can it logically be faith alone that saves if the faith that saves is never alone? The syllogism has been transmitted for so long and accepted without assessment by so many that it is tempting to affirm it, but upon close inspection we can see that the syllogism cannot logically cohere.

Joseph Dillow[230] makes a profound case that the syllogism cannot effectively separate faith and works in the requirements of eternal life. He points out that the typical reformed argument seeks to differentiate between a "condition" for justification and a "necessary result" of justification. In other words, the argument says that works are in no way a condition of justification, in that God does not take them into account in justification. However, they *are* a necessary result of justifying faith, and if they are absent it proves that the faith was not, in fact, justifying.

To inquire into the validity of the logic, it is worthwhile to shift it away from metaphysical concepts like justification to a more concrete example. Birth, Dillow argues, is a condition of growing old. Once a person is born, they will get hungry, and eating is a result of birth that is certainly necessary in order for a person to grow old. A person is responsible for eating; they may choose to do so or not. However, under the syllogism, it may be stated,

---

[230] See Joseph C. Dillow, *Reign of the Servant Kings*, 232-234

"It is birth alone that causes old age, but the birth that causes old age is never alone."

This seems absurd on the surface. If a person does not eat, they will not grow old; rather, they will die. The argument then says that eating is a "necessary result" of birth rather than a condition of old age. Dillow concisely answers this assumption:

> Here we can lay down a self-evident principle: a necessary result for which we are responsible which must be present for another result to occur is no different than an additional condition for the achievement of that second result. In the analogy of physical birth, there are therefore two conditions necessary for growing old, birth and eating, the former making the latter possible and the latter making old age possible. There is no difference between a result for which we are responsible and a condition![231]

Therefore, we can see from a more concrete example that the practical syllogism fails to deliver the desired result of making works surely present without making them a grounds for justification. Logically, if faith alone saves, then the faith that saves must be truly alone.

Continuing in our logical analysis of the practical syllogism, we must also analyze whether the syllogism makes logical sense of the cause-effect relationship between works and saving faith. Again it will be helpful to transition from abstracts to more concrete examples. Consider the equivalent to the practical syllogism, "If it rains, the streets will be wet."[232] Now certainly we can assert that if it rains, the streets will be wet. However, can we analyze whether or not it rained by looking at whether the streets are wet? Gordon Clark breaks down the logical analysis for us:

> "A little consideration will show that there are two corresponding fallacies. First, asserting the consequent; second, denying the antecedent.

---

[231] Joseph C. Dillow, *Reign of the Servant Kings*, 233

[232] We are very grateful to Fred Lybrand for this helpful analogy, as well as the analysis of its implications. See Lybrand, Fred *"Does Faith Guarantee Works? Rethinking the Reformation Cliché: 'It is therefore faith alone which justifies, and yet faith which justifies is not alone.'"* An unpublished doctoral dissertation submitted to Phoenix Seminary, March 2007.

1. "x" implies "y"
   "y" is true
   ∴ "x" is true
2. "x" implies "y"
   "x" is false
   ∴ "y" is false[233]

The first fallacy is fairly easy to see in our analogy. Our analogy stated that if it rains, the streets will be wet, but the fallacy would be to say that if the streets are wet, then it has rained. There could be any number of reasons the streets are wet (i.e. a broken dam, street sweepers, watering trucks, etc.) that do not involve rain, so asserting the consequent is not allowed. "Denying the antecedent" is just as easily shown as fallacious. "If it rains ("x"), the streets will be wet ("y"). It did not rain ("x" is false) therefore the streets are not wet ("y" is false)." We can see that, because there are many reasons the streets could be wet that do not involve rain, we cannot say that a lack of rain leads to streets that are not wet.

Can we apply this analysis of logic to the practical syllogism? The biblical texts give us several reasons to follow our logical analysis above. Jesus makes this startling statement in Matthew 7:21-23:

> "Not everyone who says to Me, 'Lord, Lord,' will enter the kingdom of heaven, but he who does the will of My Father who is in heaven will enter. "Many will say to Me on that day, 'Lord, Lord, did we not prophesy in Your name, and in Your name cast out demons, and in Your name perform many miracles?' "And then I will declare to them, 'I never knew you; depart from Me, you who practice lawlessness.'"

Certainly these people demonstrated good works. They prophesied, cast out demons, and performed many miracles in Jesus' name. By the standard of the practical syllogism we would say that their works proved that they indeed had faith. The opinion of Jesus seems at odds with this line of reasoning, in that their works proved nothing of their internal state. Jesus makes this point again in Matthew 23:27-28:

---

[233] Gordon Clark *Logic* (Jefferson, MD; The Trinity Foundation, 1985), 94-95

> "Woe to you, scribes and Pharisees, hypocrites! For you are like whitewashed tombs which on the outside appear beautiful, but inside they are full of dead men's bones and all uncleanness. "So you, too, outwardly appear righteous to men, but inwardly you are full of hypocrisy and lawlessness."

Finally, John's vision of the eternal fate of unregenerate humanity in Revelation 20:11-15 shows that the practical syllogism cannot make logical sense.

> Then I saw a great white throne and Him who sat upon it, from whose presence earth and heaven fled away, and no place was found for them. And I saw the dead, the great and the small, standing before the throne, and books were opened; and another book was opened, which is the book of life; and the dead were judged from the things which were written in the books, according to their deeds. And the sea gave up the dead which were in it, and death and Hades gave up the dead which were in them; and they were judged, every one of them according to their deeds. Then death and Hades were thrown into the lake of fire. This is the second death, the lake of fire. And if anyone's name was not found written in the book of life, he was thrown into the lake of fire.

Those whose names were not found written in the book of life were judged according to their deeds, or in the terminology we have been employing, their works. Their works did not show that they had faith; rather, their works had no connection to faith whatsoever (as evidenced by their destiny). The biblical witness is that works can absolutely be present without faith, which makes works a useless tool by which to measure faith.

Logically, then, the practical syllogism has been shown to fail the basic tests of logic. Upon close inspection we can see that making works a "necessary result" of justification is no different than making them a condition of it, which would change the gospel message into works-righteousness. We have also seen that logic dictates that using works as a gauge for faith commits either the logical error of "asserting the consequent" or "denying the antecedent." The biblical witness bears this out. Therefore, the practical syllogism has been shown to be completely untenable from a logical perspective as well as a biblical one.

We must next establish the context of our passage to provide a framework for exegesis to begin to understand the purpose of James in 2:14-26. An initial consideration is the intended audience of the epistle. Earl Radmacher chastises MacArthur's treatment of James' use of the term "brothers":

> First, MacArthur does not do justice to Hodges' claim that the warnings of James 2 cannot be directed at false professors instead of true believers. After acknowledging the presence of fifteen usages of "brethren" in James (six prefaced by "my" and three by "my beloved"), without any interaction with the usages he simply begs the question by saying that "it is common for apostolic writers to include in letters addressed to churches stern warnings for those whose profession of faith was questionable."[234]

We must heed Radmacher's advice and interact with James' usages to analyze the recipients of James. James refers to his readers as "brethren," "beloved brethren" and "my brethren." This could be taken to mean simply people of Jewish heritage. However, when we look at each use in context it becomes clear that when James speaks to his "brethren," he speaks to regenerate people.[235]

- 1:2-3: "Consider it all joy, my brethren, when you encounter various trials, knowing that the testing of your faith produces endurance." James speaks of the testing of the recipients' faith to produce endurance in their lives. This seems exceedingly odd if James were speaking to unbelievers. Even if these were people who had "spurious faith," under the Reformed maxim of perseverance these people *must* eventually fall away if they are mere professors. This would make James' comfort very misleading. Also, why would James encourage unregenerate people to endure trials? They are merely a taste of the eternal torment to

---

[234]Earl Radmacher, "First Response to 'Faith According to the Apostle James' by John F. Macarthur, Jr." *Journal of the Evangelical Theological Society Volume 33* (March 1990), 37
[235] Analysis of the use of ἀδελφοί is adapted from Robert Wilkin, "Another View of Faith and Works in James 2" *Journal of the Grace Evangelical Society 15:2* (Autumn 2002), 5-8

come. This use only makes sense if James is addressing regenerate people and offering them encouragement.

- 1:16-18: In verse 16 James calls his readers "my beloved brethren." James tells his "brethren" in verse 18, "In the exercise of His will He brought us forth by the word of truth, so that we would be a kind of first fruits among His creatures." James includes himself among those who have been brought forth by "the word of truth." The commentary tradition is unanimous that this speaks of regeneration.

- 2:1: "My brethren, do not hold your faith in our glorious Lord Jesus Christ with an attitude of personal favoritism." James could not be clearer that the "brethren" he addresses possess faith in Jesus Christ. James says "your" (i.e. the audiences') faith in "our" (i.e. held in common between James and his readers) glorious Lord Jesus Christ. If these people are simply professors and not possessors of Christ, James is being disingenuous to say the least. In fact, if these readers do not possess faith in Jesus Christ, then James is lying.

Interestingly, MacArthur does not interact with this simple yet profoundly important statement in his treatment of the passage. It is also noteworthy that the usage of ἀδελφοί is in alignment with every instance thus far in the letter. As John Hart succinctly states:

> James simply does not question the fact that his readers are true Christians. He appeals to them based on the reality of their new birth. Perhaps the most transparent statement to this effect is 2:1, "My brothers, as believers in our glorious Lord Jesus Christ, do not show favoritism" (NIV). All that James has to say is designed to shake us "as believers in our glorious Lord Jesus Christ" from the comfort of worldliness and challenge us to meet the practical needs of others such as the needs of an orphan or a widow (1:26). He does so without ever finding it necessary to scrutinize our experience of salvation.[236]

---

[236]John F. Hart. "How to Energize our Faith. Reconsidering the Meaning of James 2:14-26" *Journal of the Grace Evangelical Society Volume 12* (Spring 1999). 41

- 2:14: If James shifts his address to unregenerate people in v. 14, he certainly does so without any marker and very abruptly. This passage is the point in question, so final analysis must wait for a consideration of the remainder of the evidence. However, if James shifts usage here it is without precedent in his book and without contextual clues.
- 3:1: "Let not many of you become teachers, my brethren, knowing that as such we will incur a stricter judgment." It is inconceivable that James would tell unregenerate people that "not many of" them should teach in the church. James clearly has regenerate people in view. The judgment in view is best taken as the Bema judgment, as the context in 4:11; 5:7, 9, 10, 12 dictate. James considers himself to be under this same judgment, and it is beyond question that James was regenerate.

While it is readily admitted that unregenerate people have read James and its message both within the context of its original intended audience and throughout history, this in no way *ipso facto* proves that James was addressing unbelievers as professing but false Christians. This book, by way of analogy, is written and addressed to evangelical Christian theologians with a background in textual analysis and New Testament Greek. Others may well read it, but nevertheless the discussion and debate is addressed to those within the target demographic. Likewise, James clearly addresses the *intended* recipients of his letter as regenerate people, regardless of who else may have read it along with them. His warnings and admonitions are addressed to them *as regenerate people*, not as "so-called" or "professing" (but unregenerate) people. It is clear, then, that the "brethren" in 2:14 are regenerate people. Therefore the Lordship position that the audience James intended for his warning was unregenerate cannot withstand close scrutiny and must be discarded.

The second supposition that Lordship advocates advance is the nature of the objector's faith. James says, "What use is it, my brethren, if someone says he has faith but he has no works? Can that faith save him?" (2:14)

Lordship advocates state that the person in question only *says* he has faith.[237] Then James asks, in effect, "Can a kind of faith such as this save him?" This interpretation is built from the presence of the article on πίστις. The text states, "μὴ δύναται ἡ πίστις σῶσαι αὐτόν;" Lordship proponents argue that the article should be taken as a demonstrative pronoun (or in an anaphoric sense), i.e. *that* faith in reference to the supposed faith of the hypothetical person[238]. Therefore, according to Lordship proponents, James is discussing the *quality* of a professing believers' faith. As Bruce Compton states:

> The point is that James uses faith in a two-fold sense in these verses. More specifically, James has two kinds of faith in view, a false faith and a saving faith. The difference between the two appears to be over the matter of trust in or personal commitment to the object of faith, rather than simply the level of conviction concerning the truth about that object. The demons mentioned by James in 2:19 are convinced of the truth of what they believe, or they would not shudder at its implications. What they have not done, in contrast to what Abraham has done, is to put their trust in the true God, to commit themselves to His authority.[239]

However, James' use of the article with πίστις is nearly universal. In fact, James' only anarthrous uses of πίστις occur either in the accusation of

---

[237] So Pak, "Study of Selected Passages," 224. However, Pak does not take his analysis to its logical end. James' argument is that the person *says* they have faith. James' answer is not, "No you do not, because faith has a necessary outcome!" Rather, James' answer is, in effect, "Okay, granted your claim, can faith, which you claim (and I grant), save you?" See the discussion below regarding the anaphoric versus generic use of the article in 2:14.

[238] Daniel Wallace, *Greek Grammar Beyond the Basics*, 219, says:
> The author introduces his topic: faith without works. He then follows it with a question, asking whether this kind of faith is able to save. The use of the article both points back to a certain kind of faith as defined by the author and is used to particularize an abstract noun...the author examines two kinds of faith in 2:14–26, defining a non-working faith as a non-saving faith and a productive faith as one that saves. Both James and Paul would agree, I believe, with the statement: "Faith alone saves, but the faith that saves is not alone."

[239] R. Bruce Compton, "James 2:21-24 And The Justification Of Abraham" in *Detroit Baptist Seminary Journal Volume 2* (Fall 1997), 23

his interlocutor or within prepositional phrases. With this in mind, it is extremely unlikely that the article in this instance has demonstrative force.

Martin Dibelius , a redaction critic and certainly no flaming evangelical, has this to say about ἡ πίστις in James 2:14:

> Here Jas uses the article before "faith" (ἡ πίστις), but this is not to be read "*this* faith," as many interpreters from Bede to Mayor have argued. Jas is not speaking of any particular brand of faith… the only attributive which is expressed in ἡ πίστις is this: faith, which "has" no works. But this is still the Christian faith and not an "alleged, false faith."[240]

The other articular uses of James outside of 2:14-26 (1:3; 2:1; 5:15) are clearly definitive (i.e. generic) articles rather than demonstrative.[241] In this instance, it seems the translations of the NKJV, NRSV, and KJV are to be preferred. James also does not use modifiers on πίστις in his epistle, though MacArthur continuously qualifies and modifies "faith" in his analysis. As Radmacher points out,

> A second problem relates to MacArthur's handling of the word "faith," a word that is used sixteen times in James without ever needing a modifier. Yet the following modifiers with "faith" are sprinkled through MacArthur's paper: "counterfeit" faith, "authentic" faith, "spurious" faith, "imitation" faith, "nominal" faith, "passive" faith, "sluggish" faith, "intellectual" faith, "sensual" faith, "dead" faith, "traditional" faith, "demon" faith, "heart" faith, "spiritual" faith, "vital" faith, "transforming" faith, "personal" faith, "orthodox" faith, "actual" faith, "real" faith, "obedient" faith, "saving" faith, "efficacious" faith.[242]

---

[240] Martin Dibelius, rev. Heinrich Greeven, trans. Michael A. Williams, *A Commentary on the Epistle of James* in *Hermeneia-A Critical and Historical Commentary on the Bible* (Philadelphia; Fortress Press, 1964), 152

[241] Interestingly, even though Wallace forcefully makes his point regarding the anaphoric use of the article here, he does not analyze the additional uses in James to denote patterns in James' use. Wallace admits on page 219 that the other uses in James are simple identification, he then goes on to argue that this usage needs its own analysis. This runs perilously close to special pleading.

[242] Earl Radmacher, "First Response", 37

We should also consider the usage of πίστις in the rest of the pericope to determine if James has in mind multiple kinds of faith. In 2:20 and 22 James uses the exact same construction ἡ πίστις as is used in 2:14:

> But are you willing to recognize, you foolish fellow, that faith without works is useless? (2:20)

> You see that faith was working with his works, and as a result of the works, faith was perfected; (2:22)

In these instances it is clear that there is no anaphoric force to the article. It is only a commitment to Calvin's concept of "spurious faith" that makes the exegete look for an explanation out of the ordinary for the article in 2:14. Therefore, the argument that James is evaluating the quality of the hypothetical faith is weak at best and must be discarded. James is discussing faith, not spurious faith.

It would seem as well that the Reformed proponents do not take their analysis to its logical end. James' argument is that the person says they have faith. James does not answer, "No you do not, because faith has a necessary outcome!" Rather, James' answer is, in effect, "Okay, granted your claim to possessing faith, can faith, which you claim (and I grant), save you?" The above analysis shows that the article cannot carry demonstrative force, and as such Pak's (and others') argument that the accuser only says he has faith falls apart. Rather than arguing for two different kinds of faith, James is arguing that faith, by itself, cannot "save" someone (as James makes clear in v. 24). Pak has made the error of substituting his own answer to the question and ignoring the text's answer. Granted, as Protestants we cling tenaciously to the tenet of salvation apart from works. However, in defending that doctrine we must not bend the text to suit our tastes.

The next piece of the interpretive puzzle lies in understanding how James uses σῴζω. If faith (and not "that faith") cannot save, then what exactly does James have in mind when he discusses being saved? James uses σῴζω five times in his epistle (1:21; 2:14; 4:12; 5:15; 5:20). Looking at each one in turn shows that in context every use outside of 2:14 refers to temporal deliverance and not eternal salvation from hell.

- 1:21 reads, "Therefore, putting aside all filthiness and all that remains of wickedness, in humility receive the word implanted, which is able to save your souls." James clearly states in the immediately preceding context that he is speaking to his "beloved brethren" who have received the new birth (1:16, 19). These people were not in need of eternal deliverance, but were in need of temporal deliverance from the presence and power of sin. As Wilkins says:

> The temporal deliverance understanding of 1:21 is supported by the expression σōσαι τασ πσψχησσ ηψμōν (to save your souls). In the Septuagint and the NT this expression always or nearly always refers to the saving of one's physical life.
>
> Additionally, the readers were to receive the word "already implanted" in them, which supports the idea that they are born-again believers and that the deliverance is temporal. [243]

Wilkins argues for a temporal understanding of "salvation of the soul" with compelling evidence of its use in both the Septuagint and the New Testament.

> See for example, Mark 3:4, "Is it lawful on the Sabbath to do good or to do evil, to save life [πσψχην σωσαι] or to kill?" (Cf. Luke 6:9); "For the Son of Man did not come to destroy men's lives [πσψχησσ αντηρωπōν απολεσαι] but to save them" (Luke 9:56, MT); "There will be no loss of life [πσψχηεσ] among you, but only of the ship...Unless these men stay in the ship, you cannot be saved" (Acts 27:22, 31); "In the days of Noah...eight souls were saved [οκτō πσψχηαι διεσωτησαν] through water" (1 Pet 3:20). This expression occurs approximately eight times in the Septuagint as well, always with the sense of saving the physical life (Gen 19:17; 32:30; 1 Sam 19:11; Ps 30:7; 71:13; 109:31 [108:31 in the Septuagint]; Jer

---

[243]Wilkins, "Another View", 8-9

31:6; see also Job 33:28, which some might understand as Job hoping not to lose eternal life, but which is best understood as him hoping not to lose physical life).[244]

- 4:12 contains the next instance of σώζω. The text states, "There is only one Lawgiver and Judge, the One who is able to save and to destroy; but who are you who judge your neighbor?" God is able to save and destroy in all senses, both temporal and eternal. In the immediately following context of 4:13-17, James clearly deals with an example of the preservation of physical life, leading to the conclusion that it is preferable to see James dealing with temporal deliverance in 4:12.

- 5:15 contains an unambiguous example of temporal deliverance in James' use of σώζω: "...and the prayer offered in faith will restore the one who is sick, and the Lord will raise him up, and if he has committed sins, they will be forgiven him." Literally the text reads that the prayer of faith will "save" the sick one. It is inconceivable that eternal deliverance is in view here.

- 5:19-20: This verse provides the last use of σώζω in James.

  > My brethren, if any among you strays from the truth and one turns him back, let him know that he who turns a sinner from the error of his way will save his soul from death and will cover a multitude of sins.

This is another instance of the "save the soul" formula, and the argument above regarding the temporal nature of this phrase should guide our understanding here. Even if we don't grant that, it is also noteworthy that the wandering one is a "brother" who has "wandered away from the truth." John Niemelä comments:

---

[244]There is a possibility that the "salvation of the soul" is to be understood as in Matthew 10 and 16. There Jesus uses this as a metonymy to challenge the disciples to lose their life and joy now in order to save their life and joy in the age to come. I have defended this view of the logion in the synoptic gospels and in 1 Peter 1:9. See, Fred Chay, "A Textual and Theological Exposition on the Logion: The Salvation of the Soul." Ph.D. diss.; Trinity Theological Seminary, 2003.

> Can an unbeliever wander away from that which he has
> never believed? In the context *anyone* must be a believer,
> one of the *brethren* to whom James has now referred to
> three times as *my beloved brethren* and twelve times as *my
> brethren.*
>
> The next phrase, *and someone turns him back,*
> decisively identifies the *anyone* of this verse as a fellow
> believer. Can an unbeliever be turned back to that which
> he has never believed? The very absurdity of such a
> proposition is easily envisioned in geographic terms:
> Unless a person has been in China, how can he wander
> away from it?[245]

In light of the abundance of evidence above, unless we take James 2:14-
26 as an exception to James' otherwise unified temporal use of σῴζω (and
that with no explanatory or contextual markers), then we must concede that
the salvation in mind in 2:14-26 is the temporal deliverance from divine
discipline of a believer. Both 2:13 and 3:1 point to the judgment of believers
and form an *inclusio* around the pericope in question, framing it as dealing
with the judgment and discipline of believers. James himself expects to face
this judgment according to 3:1, which further diminishes the thought that
eternal justification is under discussion in this pericope.

Another consideration is whether James has a single justification in mind
(which Lordship advocates state must be eschatological; see MacArthur's
statements above) or multiple justifications. In other words, at the end of the
pericope James tells his readers in verse 24, "You see that a man is justified
by works and not by faith alone." (NASB) The text reads "ὁρᾶτε ὅτι ἐξ
ἔργων δικαιοῦται ἄνθρωπος καὶ οὐκ ἐκ πίστεως μόνον." Pak
summarizes the Lordship position on the nature of justification in verse 24
well:

> When James says in verse 24 ὁρᾶτε ὅτι ἐξ ἔργων
> δικαιοῦται ἄνθρωπος καὶ οὐκ ἐκ πίστεως μόνον ("you

---

[245]John Niemelä, "Faith Without Works: A Definition" *Chafer Theological Seminary Journal Volume 6* (April 2000), 11

see that a man is justified by works and not by faith
alone"), James cannot mean two different justifications (or
vindication) at the same time- one before God and one
before men. The preceding verse (v. 23) leaves no doubt
that justification before God is in view: καὶ ἐπληρώθη ἡ
γραφὴ ἡ λέγουσα, Ἐπίστευσεν δὲ Ἀβραὰμ τῷ θεῷ, καὶ
ἐλογίσθη αὐτῷ εἰς δικαιοσύνην καὶ φίλος θεοῦ ἐκλήθη
("And the Scripture was fulfilled which says, 'Abraham
believed in God and it was reckoned to him for
righteousness and he was called friend [sic] of God'").
Thus in verse 24 James is clearly teaching the
indispensability of works in justification before God not
before men.[246]

It is up to the reader to decide if the last statement above is tantamount to

a semi-Pelagian view of salvation/justification, where with the grace of God

a person can *work* to earn justification. If works are indispensable, as Pak

claims, then it would seem that eternal deliverance is not by faith *alone*, and

even the Reformed maxim "Faith alone saves, but the faith that saves is

never alone" is negated. Regardless, the Lordship position must deal with

the potentiality of conflict with Pauline soteriology at this point. As

Compton points out, "James affirms, in effect, that Abraham *was* justified by

works."[247] (emphasis original) In the next sentence he further states that this

affirmation proves that a "true, saving faith" must produce works,[248] with the

underlying assumption being that there is only a single justification in mind

in 21-24.

However, careful analysis of the text leads to the conclusion that James

does have two justifications in mind,[249] one before God (eschatological) and

another before men (temporal), which eliminates any perceived antimony

between James and Paul, maintains the integrity of James' message, and

---

[246] Joseph K. Pak, "Study of Selected Passages," 236

[247] R. Bruce Compton, "James 2:21-24," 35 See Paul Rainbow, *The Way of Salvation; The Role of Christian Obedience in Justification* and Alan P. Stanley, *Did Jesus Teach Salvation by Works?*

[248] Ibid

[249] Contra Ibid 28-29.

reiterates the unity of the Scriptures. Even Compton[250] must admit that the general agreement among scholars is that whatever justification is mentioned in verse 21, it is predicated explicitly on the *works* of Abraham, not his faith. Though Compton argues:

> Although the precise relationship between faith and works and the specific force of the compound in this verse [verse 22] is debated, it is best to take the two, faith and works, as distinct and yet related. James does not argue that the two are synonymous, only that works are the necessary *fruit* of a true, saving faith (cf. 2:14–20).[251]

His logic fails. James does not state that Abraham's works were the *result* or the *fruit* of his faith; simple observance of the text tells us that Abraham's faith was *working alongside his works*. The text reads ἡ πίστις συνήργει τοῖς ἔργοις αὐτοῦ, and BDAG lists the definition of συνεργέω as "to engage in cooperative endeavor."[252] James could not be more explicit that Abraham's justification in verse 21 was predicated on *works*, or even more specifically upon a *synergy* of works and faith, and any finessing of the text to make his works a showing or "fruit" simply ignores the plain statement of the text. If this is speaking of eschatological justification before God, then the text says that justification is based on faith and works, which is the semi-Pelagian and Catholic view, but is clearly not the clear teaching of Scripture.

The key to the interpretation of this verse lies within the word μόνον in verse 24, translated "alone" by the NASB (as well as by NKJV, ESV, and most others). At issue is whether μόνον is acting in an adjectival or adverbial manner. In other words, is μόνον acting as an adjective and

---

[250] Ibid, 36
[251] Ibid, 38
[252] BDAG, s.v. συνεργέω. TDNT calls this word "cooperation" or "aid." Liddell and Scott list "work together with, cooperate."

therefore modifying πίστεως, or is it an adverb that is modifying

δικαιοῦται? Niemelä summarizes the difficulty with the adjectival use:

> The adjectival use expresses the view that justification
> does not occur by faith alone. Rather, it is by faith and
> works. This clashes with Paul's doctrine of eternal
> justification. Advocates of this view must finesse the
> difficulty by saying that James knew that justification is by
> faith alone, but that the kind of faith that justifies is never
> alone. Faith alone is the basis for the person receiving
> eternal justification, but advocates of the view would deny
> that any workless person ever receives eternal justification.
> Another way of saying it is that both faith and works must
> be present at eternal justification, but God only takes faith
> into account at that moment.[253]

The adverbial use, on the other hand, sees μόνον as an adverb modifying

δικαιοῦται, and therefore James' message may be stated as follows: "You

see that a man is justified by works, and not [justified] only by faith." In

English, "alone" is a somewhat ambiguous term, in that it can be used as

either an adjective ("justified by faith alone," i.e. by faith by itself) or as an

adverb ("justified only by faith," i.e. justified in a singular manner, namely

by faith). The ambiguity at hand arises in that in the accusative neuter

singular, the adjective μόνος appears identically to the adverb μόνον. This

matches the English word "only," which can be used in either an adverbial or

adjectival manner depending on the context.

Because of the declination of the Greek, we can begin to tell if μόνον is

acting adjectivally by looking for a substantive within the sentence that

agrees with μόνον.[254] Even if there is a noun which agrees within the

---

[253]John Niemelä, "James 2:24: Retranslation Required (Part 1 of 3)." *Chafer Theological Seminary Journal Volume 7* (January 2001), 19. The concept of two Justifications has been articulated by D.M. Panton in the 19th century in *The Judgment Seat of Christ* (Haysville, NC.; Schoettle Publishing Co., 1984). See also Matrin Dibelius, *James* and R.T. Kendall, *Justification by Works; How Works Vindicate True Faith* (Carlisle, Great Britain; Paternoster Press, 2001)

[254] John Niemelä, "James 2:24: Retranslation Required Part 2 of 2," *Chafer Theological Seminary Journal Volume 7* (April 2001), 3

sentence, that does not automatically necessitate that μόνον is acting as an adjective. We must do further analysis to decide these cases.[255] In the case of James 2:24, Niemelä correctly summarizes:

> Despite a separation of the negative and *monon*, the verse contains no word that can agree with *monon* in case-gender-number. It is adverbial... Thus, the following translation is untenable:
>
> *A man is justified by works, and not by **faith only**.*
>
> Rather, the word *only* is adverbial.
>
> *A man is justified by works, and **not only** [**justified**] by faith.*
>
> This in turn is more easily understood as:
> A man is not only justified by faith, but also by works.[256]

What Niemelä's analysis shows is that James has a concept of two justifications, one which is before God on the basis of faith (which his quotation of Genesis 15:6 in verse 23 makes clear), and another that is on the basis of works and is before men (as his argument in verses 22, 23, and 25 make clear). Even Compton, who clearly sees James from the Reformed perspective, identifies μόνον in this verse as an adverb, and acknowledges that μόνον acting adjectivally would be a rare and little-seen use.[257] Seen in this manner, then, James' message becomes very clear: faith with no accompanying works has no value for experiential living of the Christian life.

Excursus 2: The Problem of the Jacobean interlocutor

What of the words of James' objector? James introduces an imaginary objector in verse 18, and the limitations of the words of the objector as well

---

[255] Ibid, 9
[256] Ibid, 13
[257] R. Bruce Compton, "James 2:21-24", 42-43

as James' answer are critical issues for understanding this passage. We may

dub this challenge "the problem of the interlocutor." James introduces an

opponent in verse 18, and the issue of where the objector's comments end

and James' begin is potentially the *crux interpretum* of the entire passage of

2:14-26. As Kurt Richardson cautions us, "This is a notoriously difficult

passage to translate because of the lack of punctuation in the Greek text."[258]

Not only is the lack of punctuation an issue, but verse 18 is littered with

textual variants. As John DelHousaye puts it, "although the textual

corruption is relatively minor surrounding v 18, the interlocution suffers

considerably at the hands of the copyists."[259] There are no less than seven

textual variants within this single verse, which should give the textual critic

great pause. It would appear that the copyists suffered the same difficulties

as modern commentators in determining the intent of James in this verse,

which demands a careful and thorough study! The passage reads as follows:

Ἀλλ' ἐρεῖ τις, Σὺ πίστιν ἔχεις, κἀγὼ ἔργα ἔχω· δεῖξόν μοι

τὴν πίστιν σου χωρὶς τῶν ἔργων, κἀγώ σοι δείξω ἐκ τῶν ἔργων

μου τὴν πίστιν.[260]

The variants mainly deal with the presence or absence of the personal

pronouns; however, there is a variant with the word χωρὶς, "without" that is

salient to the discussion of this difficult passage, and may shed light into the

heated discussion of Lordship salvation in this pericope.

The textual apparatus reads as follows for the variant:

Εκ 𝔓⁵⁴ᵛⁱᵈ 𝔐; Cass : *txt* ℵ B P Ψ 33. 81. 614. 630. 1241. 1505. 1739
al latt sy co

---

[258]Kurt A. Richardson, *James*, volume 36 of *The New American Commentary* (Nashville, TN: Broadman & Holman Publishers, 2001), 133 footnote 48

[259] John DelHousaye, "The Problem of the Jacobean Interlocutor" (unpublished research paper done for the author as a teaching assistant), 4

[260] Kurt and Barbara Aland, Johannes Karavidopoulos, Carlo M. Martini and Bruce Metzger, *Novum Testamentum Graece* (Stuttgart; German Bible Society, 1993), s.v. James 2:18; hereafter NA²⁷.

The reading εκ is supported by the Majority Text and $\mathfrak{P}^{54}$, though the reading cannot be determined with certainty as shown from the siglum vid. Kurt and Barbara Aland assign $\mathfrak{P}^{54}$ to their third category of manuscript weight: "Manuscripts of a distinctive character with an independent text, usually important for establishing the original text, but particularly important for the history of the text."[261] It is a papyrus of the 5th or 6th century. Cassiodorus was a Latin church father in the late 6th Century who was the private secretary of Theodoric the Great. It is doubtful that Cassiodorus knew Greek.[262] He probably possessed a Latin text no longer extant today. There also appear to be a few additional manuscripts that read εκ, as pointed out by Hodges:

> A careful count of the cursive manuscripts cited in the
> eighth edition of Merk reveals that—exclusive of his H
> and K recensions—there remain forty-nine manuscripts
> from his groups Ca, Cb, and Cc which read εκ leaving at
> the most but twenty-two from the same families attesting
> χωρις.[263] Inasmuch as Merk's C, (Caesarean) recension is
> roughly equivalent to von Soden's I class, it would appear
> probable that we should now update the critical apparati
> which here follow von Soden so as to indicate hereafter
> that the majority from this fluid grouping cohere with the
> Byzantine in support of εκ.[264]

The reading χωρὶς is supported by א B P Ψ 33. 81. 614. 630. 1241. 1505. 1739, and some manuscripts not explicitly mentioned (as shown by the siglum *al*, which represents more than the few manuscripts of *pc*).[265] Sinaiticus (א) and Vaticanus (B) are the two manuscripts of greatest import here, being fourth century uncials of the first order.

---

[261] Kurt and Barbara Aland, *The Text of the New Testament*, trans. Erroll F. Rhodes (Grand Rapids, MI; Eerdmans, 1989), 159-160

[262] Evidence for this includes the fact that Clement of Alexandria's *Hypotyposeis* was translated into Latin for him. See ibid, 177

[263] *Novum Testamentum Graece et Latine*, apparatu critico instructum edidit Augustinus Merk S.J., editio octava, 1957.

[264] Zane Hodges; "Light on James Two From Textual Criticism" in *Bibliotheca Sacra 120* (October 1963), 346

[265] NA^{27}, 56

It would seem χωρὶς has somewhat earlier attestation, as א and B are both fourth-century manuscripts and 𝔓[54] is from the 6th century. If Cassiodorus could be shown to be using an old Latin manuscript (possibly as old as the 2nd century) the scales would tip significantly, but this is not possible at this time. Χωρὶς also boasts of Alexandrian geography. Ἐκ dominates the Byzantine text-type, including per Hodges' discussion above the "Caesarean" manuscripts. Cassiodorus preserves a Western reading. Though the Byzantine readings have been much maligned as late, conflate, and therefore useless in textual criticism, there are persuasive arguments for viewing the Byzantine tradition as an early, independent witness to the autographs.[266] It would seem in light of these facts that external evidence is not decidedly for either reading. Therefore, internal evidence should be allowed to tip the scales.

Paul Wegner sets forth the principles that should be followed when determining the more probable original reading when dealing with textual variants:[267]

1. Manuscripts must be weighed, not counted.
2. Determine the reading that would most likely give rise to the others.
3. The more difficult reading is preferable.

---

[266] See Harry A. Sturtz, *The Byzantine Text-Type & New Testament Textual Criticism* (Nashville, TN; Thomas Nelson, 1984) for a thorough and persuasive discussion of the independence of the Byzantine tradition. This book was originally published as his Th.D. dissertation at Grace Theological Seminary in 1967. Though Sturtz has been misrepresented as a "Byzantine-priority" proponent (Paul Wegner, in his book *A Student's Guide to Textual Criticism of the Bible* [Downer's Grove, IL; Intervarsity Press, 2006] lists Sturtz as a Byzantine-priority scholar on page 239), his argument does not posit Byzantine *priority*. Rather Sturtz argues that the sides of the debate have inaccurately and unfairly polarized into the King James-only camp and the abandonment of the Byzantine tradition completely. He argues that "conflate" readings are not the sole property of the Byzantine family, and can be found in Alexandrian and Western witnesses as well. His main point in his book is that there are a great number of distinctively Byzantine readings (i.e. readings found in the Byzantine tradition and contradicted in Western and/or Alexandrian witnesses) that are supported from papyri readings into the second century, which should lead the textual critic to consider distinctively Byzantine readings as potentially original readings, and not dismiss them out of hand based on principles of Wescott and Hort that have since proven untenable. His work should be read by any budding textual critic as a counterbalance to the modern tendency towards abandonment of the Byzantine family altogether.
[267] Paul Wegner, *A Student's Guide to Textual Criticism*, 248

4. The shorter reading is preferable.
5. Determine which reading is more appropriate in its context.

We have already weighed the manuscript evidence and found the scales fairly evenly weighted. Which reading would most likely give rise to the others? Χωρὶς occurs 4 times in NA^{27}, including the variant at hand (2:18, 20, 26 (twice)). It is limited to James' treatise on faith and works, the pericope of 2:14-26. Ἐκ, on the other hand, occurs 13 times (2:16, 18, 21, 22, 24 (twice), 25; 3:10, 11, 13; 4:1; 5:20 (twice)). The phrase χωρὶς τῶν ἔργων occurs in verse 20 as well as in verse 26 (without the article). Since both χωρὶς and εκ occur frequently in this pericope, either is a possible reading. However, it would seem that if a scribe were to make an unintentional error in copying, he would be more likely to copy the phrase χωρὶς τῶν ἔργων from verse 20 than substitute εκ, which has no parallel in the epistle. Therefore the reading of εκ commends itself to principle number 2 above.

Which reading is more difficult? This section of James has been one of the thorniest interpretive sections in all of the New Testament, as summarized by Ron Blue:

> Few books of the Bible have been more maligned than the little Book of James. Controversy has waged over its authorship, its date, its recipients, its canonicity, and its unity. It is well known that Martin Luther had problems with this book. He called it a "right strawy epistle." But it is only "strawy" to the degree it is "sticky." There are enough needles in this haystack to prick the conscience of every dull, defeated, and degenerated Christian in the world.[268]

---

[268] J. Ronald Blue, "James" in Walvoord, John F., Roy B. Zuck, and Dallas Theological Seminary. *The Bible Knowledge Commentary : An Exposition of the Scriptures.* (Wheaton, IL: Victor Books, 1983-c1985), vol. 2, 815

It would seem that εκ is clearly the more difficult reading. Χωρὶς definitely makes the reader pause as to the objection of the interlocutor, to the point that J.B. Mayor contended that the interlocutor is an ally of James and supports his thesis.[269] However, εκ is also difficult, in that the accuser then is saying, "Show me your faith from works, and I will show you, from my works, my faith." It becomes difficult to see the actual objection. Therefore it seems that εκ is a more difficult reading, though even χωρὶς has tied evangelical scholars in interpretive knots.

Which reading is more appropriate in context? Part of the difficulty with this passage lies in the delimitation of the words of the interlocutor. James begins the remarks of his objector with the phrase Ἀλλ᾽ ἐρεῖ τις, a common diatribal marker. Hodges notes the parallel of ὦ ἄνθρωπε κενέ, "you foolish man" (v 20) with ἄφρων in 1 Cor 15:36, where Paul begins his rebuttal of his accuser.[270] There is no clear change of thought until verse 20, and though translations abound as to the *terminus* of the accusers' words,[271] verse 20 makes the most natural place. The first clear change of thought occurs in verse 20, which commends it as the end of the quote of the interlocutor.

How does this help us with the textual variant? If all of verses 18 and 19 are the words of the objector, then χωρὶς does not make good contextual sense (Perhaps this is an underlying reason why many modern translations end the interlocution earlier). However, if we substitute εκ, then the passage can contextually adhere together. The interlocutor, in effect, is arguing that a person's works and their faith are not discernible from one another. Verse 19 bears this out; in effect he says "You confess *Shema* and as a result do well. The demons also confess *Shema* (of course they know the truth of it!)

---

[269] J.B. Mayor, *The Epistle of James* (Grand Rapids, MI; Kregel Publications, 1913), 99-100
[270] Zane Hodges, "Light on James Two," 343
[271] NIV, RSV, NRSV, NKJV, NAB, NLT and the NET Bible all place the quotations after the first ἔργα ("works"); NASB, Phillips, and NCV extend it to the second ἔργων.

and their response is to shudder." Verse 18, then, argues something like this: "You have your faith, while I just have my works. Show me what you believe by what you do (which you can't- a use of the *reductio ad absurdium* argument), and I'll show what I do by what I believe (which I can't)." The two arguments coalesce into a single coherent whole.

The final principle of textual criticism listed above is not applicable in this case (neither reading is shorter). Final analysis of this passage then, leads to the following conclusions based upon the evidence:

1. Manuscript evidence is fairly even.
2. From contextual markers, ἐκ is more likely to have given rise to χωρὶς than the reverse. Therefore ἐκ is to be preferred.
3. Εκ is the more difficult reading.
4. Neither reading is shorter.
5. Contextually ἐκ makes sense of the extended interlocution and avoids the logical problems and interpretational issues of χωρὶς.

Based upon the evidence, then, ἐκ is the reading that is preferred and should be adopted. Though the *Textus Receptus* did not contain this variant and very likely contributed to its removal from modern English translations (with their dependence upon the AV for their translational history), we should view ἐκ as original and relegate χωρὶς to the status of a gloss from verse 20. Using UBS standards, I would suggest including ἐκ in the text and giving it a rating of "C"[272] to show the difficulty of the reading as well as the uncertainty inherent in the large numbers of variants in this verse.

By analyzing the words of the interlocutor, it becomes apparent that the accusation encompasses all of verses 18 and 19, and James' rebuttal begins in verse 20. This greatly assists the reader in understanding James' intent. The accuser, in effect, argues that it is impossible to link a person's belief system to their behavior, as evidenced by the divergent activities of demons

---

[272] Barbara Aland et. al., eds. *The Greek New Testament*, 4th ed. (UBS⁴) (Stuttgart; The German Bible Society, 1998), introduction, 3*

and James that are based on the same belief. James counters that works are a vital part of our belief system, in that they make faith vital and useful for today. Works "justify" a person before others, and put hands and feet to our belief system.

The temporal deliverance view has the benefit of consistent hermeneutical principles, a thorough and consistent usage of terms in the entire epistle, and a ready and straightforward explanation of the apparent (though unfounded) contradiction with Pauline soteriology. The deliverance view, in light of the word studies and contextual analysis above, sees James 2:14-26 in this light:

- Verse 14: James argues that a faith that is devoid of works cannot deliver a person from the trials and discipline that occur in this life.

- Verses 15-17 provide an example of this workless faith. If our faith is not energized by works, it has no profit.

- Verses 18-19 form the words of an interlocutor who challenges James' supposition that our faith is made mature by works.

- Verses 20-22 point to the futility of the argument. There is more to life than eternal deliverance! Verse 22 tells us that in James' mind, our faith is matured (a natural and often-seen interpretation of τελειόω[273]) by a life characterized by active obedience.

- Verses 23-26 form the final example of James' point. In verse 24, James tells us that Abraham was justified by works, and not only by faith (taking the adverb μόνον as modifying the verb δικαιοῦται). Likewise, Rahab the harlot was justified by her faithful hiding and sending out of the spies. The justification in mind is not eternal life with God, but experiential righteousness

---

[273] See John Hart, "How to Energize Our Faith", footnote 19

and witness before the world. James sums up his point by
reminding his readers that just like a corpse is animated by a
spirit, so works animate faith.

In light of the above analysis, viewing James 2 as a "test of faith" is a
complete misappropriation of the text. The context, the intended audience,
the use of terms, and the use of a consistent hermeneutic throughout the
epistle all point us to a temporal deliverance view of this debated pericope.
It would seem that Dr. Macarthur has come under his own condemnation for
depending too much on a preconceived theology and a Reformed dogma of
the perseverance of the saints, and too little on the hermeneutical spiral and
sound exegesis to determine the interpretation of this passage. James is not
telling us how to tell if we are a Christian; he is telling us, as Christians, how
to energize our faith and make it useful in the here and now.

Conclusion

There are many today who would deny the faith. There are those who would add works to faith. However, the issues we are examining and evaluating are those which alter, adjust and unknowingly amend the biblical meaning of faith itself. There is a danger in all three attitudes. For any exegetical activity or theological action that takes away from or adds to the simplicity of faith alone in Christ alone decreases, diminishes, distorts and ultimately destroys the grace of God. It comes in two manifestations. The Arminian form clearly and unashamedly requires a self activated faith and continued commitment of the penitent. However, the same result is surprisingly seen in the Calvinistic form in that while holding to the sovereignty of God and the deadness of man, it is required that a man through regeneration manifest a faith that works which is to validate and even verify the presence of saving faith.[274] It is an unintended consequence but a consequence nevertheless that man is saved by faith and unmerited works and can be assured only as long as works persist.[275] This formula

---

[274] The present study is not meant to be a primarily a theological study. It is in fact meant to be more focused on the lexical, semantic and exegetical study of the nature of faith in the New Testament. However, for a detailed exposition of the danger of the reformed Puritan expression of Calvinism see Norman Shepherd, *The Call of Grace: How the Covenant Illuminates Salvation and Evangelism* (Phillipsburg, N. J.: P&R Publishing, 2000). "Reason and Specifications Supporting the Action of the Board of Trustees in Removing Professor Shepherd: Approved by the Executive Committee of the Board, February 26, 1982," reprinted in John W. Robbins, *A Companion to the Current Justification Controversy* (Unicoi, TN: The Trinity Foundation, 2003), 136. Norman Shepherd, "The Grace of Justification" (paper presented to the Board of Trustees of Westminster Theological Seminary, Philadelphia, Pa., 8 February, 1979). An electronic version of this document is available online at http://www.hornes.org/theologia/ content/norman_shepherd/the_grace_of_justification.htm, a website maintained by Shepherd supporter Rev. Mark Horne. Norman Shepherd, "Thirty-Four Theses on Justification in Relation to Faith, Repentance, and Good Works" (paper presented to the Board of Trustees of Westminster Theological Seminary, Philadelphia, Pa., 8 February, 1979). An electronic version of this document is also available online at http://www.hornes.org/theologia/content/ norman_shepherd/the_34_theses.htm. Edmund P. Clowney, "Controversial Issues in the Teaching of Professor Shepherd" (paper presented to the visitation committee to Westminster Theological Seminary, Philadelphia, Pa., 11 November, 1981). A more modern expression and articulation of the activistic nature of faith is seen in Daniel Fuller's *Unity of the Bible* and adopted by John Piper in *Future Grace*.

[275] For those who anticipated these dangers on theological grounds seen through the view of historical theology and its pastoral consequences see the previously listed works of R.T. Kendall, M. Charles Bell and Michael Eaton

seems to be little different than being saved by faith that must produce or result in works, for it actually can be articulated that a person must manifest works to be saved. It is to reduce the Reformation ideal of Sola Gracea to a synergistic understanding of salvation similar to the Roman Catholic theology evidenced in the council of Trent.[276]

Calvin in response to the Council of Trent by way of "The Antidotes" coined, "We are saved by faith alone but the faith that saves is never alone". [277] If we are to articulate that we are saved by faith alone and then stipulate by definition that the faith that saves is never alone, it seems difficult to then pronounce that we are saved by faith alone, since by definition faith is never alone. The law of non-contradiction refuses to yield to the "sleep of reason" for it can only bring forth monsters- both philosophical and theological.[278]

It is the sign of an educated mind to be able to entertain a thought without accepting it.[279] This study has attempted to entertain a thought but has not been convinced from scripture that it is acceptable. The present work is not

---

[276] At this point the fallacious charge of antinomian is often leveled. However if what the standard dictionary definition is meant by the term we heartily confess to being guilty. According to Merriam-Webster online dictionary Antinomian- Etymology: Medieval Latin *antinomus,* from Latin *anti-* + Greek *nomos* law
1 : one who holds that under the gospel dispensation of grace the moral law is of no use or obligation because faith alone is necessary to salvation.

[277] Calvin in response to the Council of Trent canon 11 in his Antidotes to Trent. We are indebted to Fred Lybrand for making this citation available. " I wish the reader to understand that as often as we mention Faith alone in this question, we are not thinking of a dead faith, which worketh not by love, but holding faith to be the only cause of justification. (Galatians 5:6; Romans 3:22.) It is therefore faith alone which justifies, and yet the faith which justifies is not alone: just as it is the heat alone of the sun which warms the earth, and yet in the sun it is not alone, because it is constantly conjoined with light. Wherefore we do not separate the whole grace of regeneration from faith, but claim the power and faculty of justifying entirely for faith, as we ought. And yet it is not us that these Tridentine Fathers anathematize so much as Paul, to whom we owe the definition that the righteousness of man consists in the forgiveness of sins. The words are in the fourth chapter to the Romans, "David speaketh of the blessedness of the man to whom God imputeth righteousness without works, saying, Blessed are those whose iniquities are forgiven." (Psalm 32:1) We see that in Paul's view blessedness and righteousness mean the same thing. And where does he place both but solely in the remission of sins?

[277] See Lybrand, Fred *"Does Faith Guarantee Works? Rethinking the Reformation Cliché: 'It is therefore faith alone which justifies, and yet faith which justifies is not alone.'"* An unpublished doctoral dissertation submitted to Phoenix Seminary, March 2007.

[278] The novel *The Sleep of Reason* by C.P. Snow attributes this quote to Goya but the source is unknown.

[279] This is anecdotally attributed to Aristotle.

meant to be a theological or pastoral treatise but it is self evident that both pastoral and systematic theology must be informed and influenced concerning the meaning of such a critical term as Faith in the New Testament.

Much of what is written in today's Christian market can be relegated to be nothing more than "amusing irrelevance". It is banal to the core. Such is not the case in this study for this issue concerns eternal life or eternal death. The apostolic answer to the Philippian jailer could not have been clearer, " What must I do to be save? Believe on the Lord Jesus Christ and you shall be saved."

Postlude

The past will not tell us what we ought to do, but it will often tell us what we ought to avoid. Traditions are the tramways of intellectual transportation.[280] And yet traditions are not to be assumed automatically or assimilated uncritically. Theological traditions like all dogma are to be open to inspection and if necessary, rejection. I fear that within evangelical theology in some ways we do not know what is happening to us, and this is precisely what is happening to us— not to know what is happening to us.

---

[280] Jose Ortega y Gasset

Appendix 1

πιστεύω in the NT	
Indicative	Non – Indicative
Matthew 8:13	Matthew 18:6
Matthew 9:28	Matthew 21:22
Matthew 15:32	Matthew 21:32
Matthew 21:25	Matthew 24:23
Matthew 21:32	Matthew 24:26
Mark 9:24	Mark 1:15
Mark 11:31	Mark 5:36
Mark 16:13	Mark 9:23
Mark 16:14	Mark 9:42
Luke 1:20	Mark 11:23
Luke 8:13	Mark 11:24
Luke 16:11	Mark 13:21
Luke 20:5	Mark 15:32
John 1:50	Mark 16:16
John 2:11	Mark 16:17
John 2:22	Luke 1:45
John 2:23	Luke 8:12
John 2:24	Luke 8:50
John 3:12	Luke 22:67
John 3:18	Luke 24:25
John 4:39	John 1:7
John 4:41	John 1:12
John 4:42	John 3:15
John 4:50	John 3:16
John 4:53	John 3:18 (twice)
John 5:38	John 3:36
John 5:46	John 4:21
John 5:47	John 4:48
John 6:36	John 5:24
John 6:64	John 5:44
John 6:69	John 6:29
John 7:5	John 6:30
John 7:31	John 6:35
John 7:48	John 6:40
John 8:30	John 6:47
John 8:45	John 6:64
John 8:46	John 7:38
John 9:18	John 7:39
John 9:35	John 8:24
John 9:38	John 8:31
John 10:25	John 9:36
John 10:26	John 10:37

John 10:42	John 10:38
John 11:26	John 11:15
John 11:27	John 11:25
John 11:45	John 11:26
John 11:48	John 11:40
John 12:11	John 11:42
John 12:37	John 12:36
John 12:38	John 12:39
John 12:42	John 12:44
John 12:44	John 12:46
John 14:10	John 13:19
John 16:9	John 14:1 (twice)
John 16:27	John 14:11(twice)
John 16:30	John 14:12
John 16:31	John 14:29
John 17:8	John 17:20
John 20:8	John 17:21
John 20:29	John 20:25
Acts 4:4	John 20:29
Acts 8:12	John 20:31
Acts 8:13	Acts 2:44
Acts 9:42	Acts 4:32
Acts 13:12	Acts 5:14
Acts 13:48	Acts 9:26
Acts 14:23	Acts 10:43
Acts 15:11	Acts 11:17
Acts 17:12	Acts 11:21
Acts 17:34	Acts 13:39
Acts 18:8	Acts 13:41
Acts 26:27 (twice)	Acts 14:1
Acts 27:25	Acts 15:5
Romans 3:2	Acts 15:7
Romans 4:3	Acts 16:31
Romans 4:17	Acts 16:34
Romans 4:18	Acts 18:27
Romans 6:8	Acts 19:2
Romans 10:10	Acts 19:4
Romans 10:14	Acts 19:18
Romans 10:16	Acts 21:20
Romans 13:11	Acts 21:25
Romans 14:2	Acts 22:19
1 Corinthians 3:5	Acts 24:14
1 Corinthians 9:17	Romans 1:16
1 Corinthians 11:18	Romans 3:22
1 Corinthians 13:7	Romans 4:5

1 Corinthians 15:2	Romans 4:11
1 Corinthians 15:11	Romans 4:24
2 Corinthians 4:13	Romans 9:33
Galatians 2:7	Romans 10:4
Galatians 2:16	Romans 10:9
Galatians 3:6	Romans 10:11
1 Thessalonians 4:14	Romans 10:14
2 Thessalonians 1:10	Romans 15:13
1 Timothy 1:11	1 Corinthians 1:21
1 Timothy 3:16	1 Corinthians 14:22 (twice)
2 Timothy 1:12	Galatians 3:22
Titus 1:3	Ephesians 1:13
James 2:19	Ephesians 1:19
James 2:23	Philippians 1:29
1 John 4:16	1 Thessalonians 1:7
1 John 5:10	1 Thessalonians 2:4
	1 Thessalonians 2:10
	1 Thessalonians 2:13
	2 Thessalonians 1:10
	2 Thessalonians 2:11
	2 Thessalonians 2:12
	1 Timothy 1:16
	Titus 3:8
	Hebrews 4:3
	Hebrews 11:6
	1 Peter 1:8
	1 Peter 2:6
	1 Peter 2:7
	1 John 3:23
	1 John 4:1
	1 John 5:1
	1 John 5:5
	1 John 5:10 (twice)
	1 John 5:13
	Jude 5

Appendix 2: New Testament Occurrences of πείθω

Matthew 27:20	Romans 8:38
Matthew 27:43	Romans 14:14
Matthew 28:14	Romans 15:14
Luke 11:22	2 Corinthians 1:9
Luke 16:31	2 Corinthians 2:3
Luke 18:9	2 Corinthians 5:11
Luke 20:6	2 Corinthians 10:7
Acts 5:36	Galatians 1:10
Acts 5:37	Galatians 5:7
Acts 5:39	Galatians 5:10
Acts 12:20	Philippians 1:6
Acts 13:43	Philippians 1:14
Acts 14:19	Philippians 1:25
Acts 17:4	Philippians 2:24
Acts 18:4	Philippians 3:3
Acts 19:8	Philippians 3:4
Acts 19:26	2 Thessalonians 3:4
Acts 21:14	2 Timothy 1:5
Acts 23:21	2 Timothy 1:12
Acts 26:26	Philemon 21
Acts 26:28	Hebrews 2:13
Acts 27:11	Hebrews 6:9
Acts 28:23	Hebrews 13:17
Acts 28:24	Hebrews 13:18
Romans 2:8	James 3:3
Romans 2:19	1 John 3:19

Appendix 3: Septuagint occurrences of πιστεύω

πιστεύω	Hebrew Root	Stem		καταπιστεύω	Hebrew Root	Stem
Gen 15:6	אמן	Hiphil		Micah 7:5	אמן	Hiphil
Gen 42:20	אמן	Niphal				
Gen 45:26	אמן	Hiphil				
Ex 4:1	אמן	Hiphil				
Ex 4:5	אמן	Hiphil		ἐμπιστεύω		
Ex 4:8 (twice)	אמן	Hiphil		Deut 1:32	אמן	Hiphil
Ex 4:9	אמן	Hiphil		Judg 11:20	אמן	Hiphil
Ex 4:31	אמן	Hiphil		2 Chron 20:20	אמן	Hiphil
Ex 14:31	אמן	Hiphil		2 Chron 20:20	אמן	Niphal
Ex 19:9	אמן	Hiphil		Jonah 3:5	אמן	Hiphil
Num 14:11	אמן	Hiphil				
Num 20:12	אמן	Hiphil				
Deut 9:23	אמן	Hiphil				
Deut 28:66	אמן	Hiphil				
1 Sam 3:21 (20 BHS/NASB)	אמן	Niphal				
1 Sam 27:12	אמן	Hiphil				
1 Ki 10:7	אמן	Hiphil				
2 Chron 9:6	אמן	Hiphil				
2 Chron 32:15	אמן	Hiphil				
Job 4:18	אמן	Hiphil				
Job 9:16	אמן	Hiphil				
Job 15:15	אמן	Hiphil				
Job 15:22	אמן	Hiphil				

Job 15:31	אָמַן	Hiphil				
Job 24:22	אָמַן	Hiphil				
Job 29:24	אָמַן	Hiphil				
Job 39:12	אָמַן	Hiphil				
Job 39:24	אָמַן	Hiphil				
Ps 26:13 (27:13 LXX)	אָמַן	Hiphil				
Ps 77:22 (78:22 LXX)	אָמַן	Hiphil				
Ps 77:32 (78:32 LXX)	אָמַן	Hiphil				
Ps 105:12 (106:12 LXX)	אָמַן	Hiphil				
Ps 105:24	אָמַן	Hiphil				
Ps 115:1	אָמַן	Hiphil				
Ps 118:66	אָמַן	Hiphil				
Prov 14:15	אָמַן	Hiphil				
Prov 30:1	אָמַן	Hiphil				
Isa 7:9	אָמַן	Hiphil				
Isa 28:16	אָמַן	Hiphil				
Isa 43:10	אָמַן	Hiphil				
Isa 53:1	אָמַן	Hiphil				
Jer 12:6	אָמַן	Hiphil				
Jer 25:8	שָׁמַע	Qal				
Jer 47:14	אָמַן	Hiphil				
Lam 4:12	אָמַן	Hiphil				
Dan 6:24	אָמַן	Haphal	Aramaic			
Hab 1:5	אָמַן	Hiphil				

Appendix 4: בָּטַח in BHS and its translation in the LXX

Reference	Benyan	LXX	LXX form
Dt 28:52	Qal Participle MSA	πείθω	Perfect Active Indicative
Jdg 9:26	Qal Impf 3MP	ἐλπίζω/πείθω	Aorist/pluperfect Active Indicative
Jdg 18:7	Qal Participle MSA	ἐλπίς	Noun Fem Sing Dative
Jdg 18:10	Qal Participle MSA	ἐλπίζω/πείθω	Perf Act Part/Noun
Jdg 18:27	Qal Participle MSA	πείθω	Perf Act Part
Jdg 20:36	Qal Perf 3CP	ἐλπίζω	Aorist Active Indicative
2 Ki 18:5	Qal Perf 3MS	ἐλπίζω	Aorist Active Indicative
2 Ki 18:19	Qal Perf 2MS	πείθω	Perfect Active Indicative
2 Ki 18:20	Qal Perf 2MS	πείθω	Perfect Active Participle
2 Ki 18:21	Qal Perf 2MS	πείθω	Perfect Active Indicative
2 Ki 18:21 #2	Qal Participle MPA	πείθω	Perfect Active Participle
2 Ki 18:22	Qal Perfect 1CP	πείθω	Perfect Active Indicative
2 Ki 18:24	Qal Impf 2MS waw consc	ἐλπίζω	Aorist Active Indicative
2 Ki 18:30	Hiph Impf 3MS	ἐπελπιζω	Present Active Imperative
2 Ki 19:10	Qal Participle MSA	πείθω	Perfect Active Indicative
1 Ch 5:20	Qal Perf 3CP	ἐλπίζω	Aorist Active Indicative
2 Ch 32:10	Qal Participle MPA	πείθω	Perfect Active Indicative
Job 6:20	Qal Perfect 3MS	πείθω	Perfect Active Participle
Job 11:18	Qal Perfect 2MS	πείθω	Perfect Active Participle
Job 39:11	Qal Imperfect 2MS	πείθω	Perfect Active Indicative
Job 40:23	Qal Imperfect 3MS	πείθω	Perfect Active Indicative
Ps 4:6	Qal Imperative 2MP	ἐλπίζω	Aorist Active Indicative
Ps 9:11	Qal Imperfect 3MP	ἐλπίζω	Aorist Active Indicative
Ps 13:6	Qal Perfect 1CP	ἐλπίζω	Aorist Active Indicative

Ps 21:8	Qal Participle MSA	ἐλπίζω	Present Active Indicative
Ps 22:5 (twice)	Qal Perfect 3CP	ἐλπίζω	Aorist Active Indicative
Ps 22:6	Qal Perfect 3CP	ἐλπίζω	Aorist Active Indicative
Ps 22:10	Hiphil Participle MSC	ἐλπίς	Noun Singular
Ps 25:2	Qal Perfect 1CS	πείθω	Perfect Active Indicative
Ps 26:1	Qal Perfect 1CS	ἐλπίζω	Present Active Participle
Ps 27:3	Qal Participle MSA	ἐλπίζω	Present Active Indicative
Ps 28:7	Qal Perfect 3MS	ἐλπίζω	Aorist Active Indicative
Ps 31:7	Qal Perfect 1CS	ἐλπίζω	Aorist Active Indicative
Ps 31:15	Qal Perfect 1CS	ἐλπίζω	Aorist Active Indicative
Ps 32:10	Qal Participle MSA	ἐλπίζω	Present Active Participle
Ps 33:21	Qal Perfect 1CP	ἐλπίζω	Aorist Active Indicative
Ps 37:3	Qal Imperative 2MS	ἐλπίζω	Aorist Active Imperative
Ps 37:5	Qal Imperative 2MS	ἐλπίζω	Aorist Active Imperative
Ps 40:4	Qal Imferfect 3MP	ἐλπίζω	Future Active Indicative
Ps 41:10	Qal Perfect 1CS	ἐλπίζω	Aorist Active Indicative
Ps 44:7	Qal Imperfect 1CS	ἐλπίζω	Future Active Indicative
Ps 49:7	Qal Participle MPA	πείθω	Perfect Active Participle
Ps 52:9	Qal Imperfect 3MS	ἐπελπιζω	Aorist Active Indicative
Ps 52:10	Qal Perfect 1CS	ἐλπίζω	Aorist Active Indicative
Ps 55:24	Qal Imperfect 1CS	ἐλπίζω	Future Active Indicative
Ps 56:4	Qal Imperfect 1CS	ἐλπίζω	Future Active Indicative
Ps 56:5	Qal Perfect 1CS	ἐλπίζω	Aorist Active Indicative
Ps 56:12	Qal Perfect 1CS	ἐλπίζω	Aorist Active Indicative
Ps 62:9	Qal Imperative 2MS	ἐλπίζω	Aorist Active Indicative
Ps 62:11	Qal Imperfect 2MP	ἐλπίζω	Present Active Indicative
Ps 78:22	Qal Perfect 3CP	ἐλπίζω	Aorist Active Indicative

Ps 84:13	Qal Participle MSA	ἐλπίζω	Present Active Participle
Ps 86:2	Qal Participle MSA	ἐλπίζω	Present Active Participle
Ps 91:2	Qal Imperfect 1CS	ἐλπίζω	Future Active Indicative
Ps 112:7	Qal Passive Participle MSA	ἐλπίζω	Present Active Infinitive
Ps 115:8	Qal Participle MSA	πείθω	Perfect Active Participle
Ps 115:9	Qal Imperative 2MS	ἐλπίζω	Aorist Active Indicative
Ps 115:10	Qal Imperative 2MP	ἐλπίζω	Aorist Active Indicative
Ps 115:11	Qal Imperative 2MP	ἐλπίζω	Aorist Active Indicative
Ps 118:8	Qal Infinitive Construct	πείθω	Perfect Active Infinitive
Ps 118:9	Qal Infinitive Construct	ἐλπίζω	Present Active Infinitive
Ps 119:42	Qal Perfect 1CS	ἐλπίζω	Aorist Active Indicative
Ps 125:1	Qal Participle MPA	πείθω	Perfect Active Participle
Ps 135:18	Qal Participle MSA	πείθω	Perfect Active Participle
Ps 143:8	Qal Perfect 1CS	ἐλπίζω	Aorist Active Indicative
Ps 146:3	Qal Imperfect 2MP	πείθω	Perfect Active Indicative
Pr 3:5	Qal Imperative 2MS	πείθω	Perfect Active Participle
Pr 11:15	Qal Participle MSA	ἀσφάλεια	Noun
Pr 11:28	Qal Participle MSA	πείθω	Perfect Active Participle
Pr 14:16	Qal Participle MSA	πείθω	Perfect Active Participle
Pr 16:20	Qal Participle MSA	πείθω	Perfect Active Participle
Pr 28:1	Qal Imperfect 2MS	πείθω	Perfect Active Indicative
Pr 28:25	Qal Participle MSA	πείθω	Perfect Active Indicative
Pr 28:26	Qal Participle MSA	πείθω	Perfect Active Indicative
Pr 29:25	Qal Participle MSA	πείθω	Perfect Active Participle
Pr 31:11	Qal Perfect 3MS	θαρσέω	Present Active Indicative
Is 12:2	Qal Imperfect 1CS	πείθω	Perfect Active Participle
Is 26:3	Qal Passive Participle MSA	ἐλπίζω	Aorist Active Indicative

Is 26:4	Qal Imperative 2MP	ἐλπίζω	Aorist Active Indicative
Is 30:12	Qal Imperfect 2MP	ἐλπίζω	Aorist Active Indicative
Is 31:1	Qal Imperfect 3MP	πείθω	Perfect Active Participle
Is 32:9	Qal Participle FPA	ἐλπίς	Noun
Is 32:10	Qal Participle FPA	ἐλπίς	Noun
Is 32:11	Qal Participle FPA	πείθω	Perfect Active Participle
Is 36:4	Qal Perfect 2MS	πείθω	Perfect Active Participle
Is 36:5	Qal Perfect 2MS	πείθω	Perfect Active Indicative
Is 36:6	Qal Perfect 2MS	πείθω	Perfect Active Participle
Is 36:7	Qal Perfect 1CP	πείθω	Perfect Active Indicative
Is 36:9	Qal Imperfect 2MS	πείθω	Perfect Active Participle
Is 36:15	Hiphil Imperfect 3MS	ῥύομαι	Future Middle Indicative
Is 37:10	Qal Participle MSA	πείθω	Perfect Active Participle
Is 42:17	Qal Participle MPA	πείθω	Perfect Active Participle
Is 47:10	Qal Imperfect 2FS	ἐλπίς	Noun
Is 50:10	Qal Imperfect 3MS	πείθω	Perfect Active Indicative
Is 59:4	Qal Infinitive Absolute	πείθω	Perfect Active Indicative
Je 5:17	Qal Participle MSA	πείθω	Perfect Active Indicative
Je 7:4	Qal Imperfect 2MP	πείθω	Perfect Active Imperative
Je 7:8	Qal Participle MPA	πείθω	Perfect Active Indicative
Je 7:14	Qal Participle MPA	πείθω	Perfect Active Indicative
Je 9:3	Qal Imperfect 2MP	πείθω	Perfect Active Imperative
Je 12:5	Qal Participle MSA	πείθω	Perfect Active Indicative
Je 13:25	Qal Imperfect 2FS	ἐλπίζω	Aorist Active Indicative
Je 17:5	Qal Imperfect 3MS	ἐλπίς	Noun
Je 17:7	Qal Imperfect 3MS	πείθω	Perfect Active Indicative
Je 23:6	Hiphil Perfect 2MS	πείθω	Perfect Active Participle

161

Je 28:15	Hiphil Perfect 2MS	πείθω	Perfect Active Participle
Je 29:31	Hiphil Imperfect 3MS	πείθω	Perfect Active Participle
Je 39:18	Qal Perfect 2MS		Not in LXX
Je 46:25	Qal Participle MPA	πείθω	Perfect Active Participle
Eze 16:15	Qal Imperfect 2FS	πείθω	Pluperfect Active Indicative
Eze 33:13	Qal Perfect 3MS	πείθω	Perfect Active Indicative
Ho 10:13	Qal Perfect 2MS	ἐλπίζω	Aorist Active Indicative
Am 6:1	Qal Participle MPA	πείθω	Perfect Active Participle
Mic 7:5	Qal Imperfect 2MP	ἐλπίζω	Present Active Indicative
Hab 2:18	Qal Perfect 3MS	πείθω	Perfect Active Indicative
Zep 3:2	Qal Perfect 3FS	πείθω	Pluperfect Active Indicative

WORKS CITED

Books:

Aland, Kurt and Barbara Aland. *The Text of the New Testament*. Trans. Erroll F. Rhodes. Grand Rapids, MI: Eerdmans, 1989

Barr, James. *The Semantics of Biblical Language*. London: Oxford University Press, 1961

Beasley-Murray, George R. *John*. Vol. 36 of *Word Biblical* Commentary. Ed. David A. Hubbard and Glenn W. Barker. Dallas, TX: Word, Inc., 2002.

Berkhof, Louis. *Systematic Theology*. Grand Rapids, MI: Eerdmans, 1996

Black, David A. *It's Still Greek to Me*. Grand Rapids, MI: Baker Book House, 1998

Blue, J. Ronald. "James" in Walvoord, John F., Roy B. Zuck, and Dallas Theological Seminary. *The Bible Knowledge Commentary : An Exposition of the Scriptures*. Wheaton, IL: Victor Books, 1983-c1985

Boice, James Montgomery. *The Gospel of John*. Grand Rapids, MI: Zondervan, 1985.

Bruce, F.F. *Galatians* in The New International Greek Testament Commentary. Grand Rapids, MI: Eerdmans, 1982

Burton, Ernest De Witt. *A critical and exegetical commentary on the Epistle to the Galatians* The International Critical Commentary [on the Holy Scriptures of the Old and New Testaments]vol. 35. Edinburgh: T&T Clark, 1921, 1950.

Calvin, John. *A Commentary on the Gospel According to John*. Trans. William Pringle. Grand Rapids, MI: Baker Books, 1981
_____. *Institutes of the Christian Religion*. Trans. Henry Beveridge. Grand Rapids, MI: Eerdmans, 1989

Carson, D. A. *Exegetical Fallacies*. 2nd ed. Grand Rapids, MI: Baker Book House, 1996
_____. *The Gospel According to John*. Grand Rapids, MI: Eerdmans, 1991.
_____., Peter O'Brien and Mark Seifrid. *Justification and Variegated Nomism*. Vol. 2. Grand Rapids, MI: Baker Academic, 2004

Chantry, Walter. *Today's Gospel: Authentic or Synthetic?* Carlisle, PA. Banner of Truth Trust, 1970

Clark, Gordon. *Logic*. Jefferson, MD: The Trinity Foundation, 1985
_____. *What is Saving Faith?* N.P.: The Trinity Foundation, 1990

Dana, H.E. and Julius R. Mantey. *A Manual of the Greek New Testament*. Toronto: The Macmillan Company, 1957

Davis, W.D. *Paul and Rabbinic Judaism*. New York: Harper, 1948

Dibelius, Martin. *A Commentary on the Epistle of James*. Rev. Heinrich Greeven. Trans. Michael A. Williams. In *Hermeneia-A Critical and*

    Historical Commentary on the Bible. Philadelphia, PA. Fortress
        Press, 1964.

Dillow, Joseph. *The Reign of the Servant Kings.* Hayesville, NC: Schoettle
    Publishing Co., 1993

Dodd, C.H. *The Interpretation of the Fourth Gospel.* Cambridge: University
    Press, 1968

Dunn, James D.G. *Romans 1-8.* vol. 38a of *Word Biblical* Commentary. Ed.
    David A. Hubbard and Glenn W. Barker. Dallas: Word Books,
    1988

Dunn, James D.G. *Romans 9-16.* vol. 38b of *Word Biblical* Commentary.
    Ed. David A. Hubbard and Glenn W. Barker. Dallas: Word Books,
    1988

_____. *Unity and Diversity in the New Testament: An Inquiry into the
    Character of Earliest Christianity.* 2nd ed. Harrisburg, PA: Trinity
    Press International, 1999

Fuller, Daniel. *The Unity of the Bible: Unfolding God's Plan for Humanity.*
    Grand Rapids, MI: Zondervan, 1992

Geisler, Norman. *Systematic Theology.* Vol. 3. *Sin and Salvation.*
    Minneapolis, MN: Bethany House, 2004

Govett, Robert. *Govett on Romans.* Haynesville, NC: Schoettle Publishing
    Company, 1981

Grudem, Wayne. *Systematic Theology.* Grand Rapids, MI: Zondervan,
    2000.

Harrison, Everett F. "Matthew" in *Expositor's Bible Comentary.* Frank E.
    Gaebelein, ed. Grand Rapids, MI: Zondervan, 1995

_____. *Romans.* Grand Rapids, MI: Zondervan, 1976

Helm, Paul. *Calvin and the Calvinists.* Carlisle, PA: Banner of Truth Trust,
    1982.

Hirsch Jr., E.D. *Validity in Interpretation.* Yale University: New Haven
    Publishers, 1967.

Hodges, Zane. *Absolutely Free: A Biblical Reply to Lordship Salvation.*
    Dallas: Redencion Viva, 1989

_____. *The Gospel Under Siege.* 2nd ed. Dallas: Redencion Viva, 1992

Husbands, Mark and Daniel J. Treier, eds. *Justification.* Downers Grove, IL:
    Intervarsity Press, 2004

Jobes, Karen and Moises Silva, *Invitation to the Septuagint.* Grand Rapids:
    Baker Books, 2000

Keener, Craig. *The Gospel of John: A Commentary.* Peabody, MA:
    Hendrickson Publishers, 2003

Kendall, R.T. *Calvin and English Calvinism to 1649.* Oxford: Oxford
    University Press, 1979.

_____. *Justification by Works: How Works Vindicate True Faith.*
    Carlisle, Great Britain: Paternoster Press, 2001.

Kim, Seyoon. *Paul and the New Perspective: Second Thoughts on the
    origins of Paul's Gospel.* Grand Rapids, MI: Eerdmans, 2002

Kostenberger, Andreas J. *John*. In *Baker Exegetical Commentary on the New Testament*. Grand Rapids, MI: Baker Publishing, 2004

Lange, J.P. and F.R. Lay. "The Epistle of Paul to the Romans." Vol. 5 of *Lange's Commentary on the Holy Scriptures*. Grand Rapids, MI: Zondervan, 1960

Lopez, Rene. *Romans Unlocked*. Springfield, MO: 21st Century press, 2005

Luther, Martin. *Commentary on the Epistle to the Galatians* (1535), trans. Theodore Graebner. Grand Rapids, MI: Zondervan Publishing House, 1949

MacArthur, John. *Faith Works: The Gospel According to the Apostles*. Word Publishing, 1993

_____. *The Gospel According to Jesus: What Does Jesus Mean When He Says, 'Follow Me'?* Grand Rapids, MI: Zondervan, 1994

Marshall, I. Howard. *Kept by the Power of God*. Paternoster Digital; 2005

Mayor, J.B. *The Epistle of James* Grand Rapids, MI: Kregel Publications, 1913

Moo, Douglas. *The Epistle to the Romans*. (Grand Rapids, MI: Eerdmans, 1996

Morris, Leon. *The Gospel According to John*. Grand Rapids, MI: Eerdmans, 1995

Moule, C.F.D. *An Idiom Book of New Testament Greek*. Cambridge: Cambridge University Press, 1959

Moulton, J.H. *A Grammar of the Greek New Testament* Vol 3. Edinburgh: T.& T Clark, 1963.

Mounce, Robert. *Romans*. Nashville, TN: Broadman and Holman, 2001

Moyer, Larry, *Free and Clear*. Grand Rapids, MI: Kregel Publications, 1997

Murray, John. "Romans" in F. F. Bruce, ed. *The New International Commentary on the New Testament*. 2 vols. In 1. Grand Rapids, MI: Eerdmans, 1965

Nygren, Anders. *Commentary on Romans*. Philadelphia: Fortress Press, 1949

Panton, D.M. *The Judgment Seat of Christ*. Haysville, NC: Schoettle Publishing Company, 1984.

Piper, John. *Desiring God*. Sisters, OR: Multnomah Publishers, 2003

_____. *Future Grace*. Sisters, OR: Multnomah Publishers, 1995

_____. *The Future of Justification* Wheaton, IL: Crossway Books, 2007

Rainbow, Paul A. *The Way of Salvation; The Role of Christian Obedience in Justification*. Bletchley, Milton Keynes, UK: Paternoster Press, 2005.

Ramm, Bernard. *Protestant Bible Interpretation: A Textbook on Hermeneutics*. 3rd ed. Grand Rapids, MI: Baker Books, 1970, quoted in Robert Thomas, "The Principle of Single Meaning." *The Master's Seminary Journal 12/1*. (Spring, 2001)

Richardson, Kurt A. *James*. Vol. 36 of *The New American Commentary*. Nashville, TN: Broadman & Holman Publishers, 2001.

Riddlebarger, Kim. "What is Faith?" in Michel Horton, ed. *Christ the Lord: The Reformation and Lordship Salvation*. Grand Rapids, MI: Baker Books, 1992

Robertson, A.T. *Grammar of the Greek New Testament: in Light of Historical Research*. Nashville, TN: Broadman & Holman Publishers, 1947

Ryrie, Charles C. *So Great Salvation*. Wheaton, IL: Victor books, 1989

Sanday, William and Arthur C. Heedlam. *A Critical and Exegetical Commentary on the Epistle to the Romans*. Grand Rapids: Zondervan, 1957

Sanders, E.P. *Paul and Palestinian Judaism*. Minneapolis, MN: Augsburg Fortress, 1977

Schaff, Philip. *The Nicene and Post-Nicene Fathers*. Vol. 5. *Saint Augustine: Anti-Pelagian Writings*. Oak Harbor, WA: Logos Research Systems, Inc., 1997. CD-ROM. Logos Bible Software, Series X.

Schreiner, Thomas and Ardel Caneday, *The Race Set before Us: A Biblical Theology of Perseverance & Assurance*. Downers Grove, IL: Intervarsity Press, 2001

_____. *Romans*. Grand Rapids, MI: Baker Book House, 1998

Shank, Robert. *Life in the Son*. Springfield, MO: Westcott Publishers, 1960

Shedd, William B.T. *A Critical and Doctrinal Commentary on the Epistle of St. Paul to the Romans*. Minneapolis, MN: Klock and Klock Christian Publishers, 1978

_____. *Dogmatic Theology*. Phillipsburg, NJ: P&R Publishing, 2005

Smalley, Stephen S. *1, 2, 3 John*. Dallas: Word, Inc., 2002

Sproul, R. C. *Faith Alone: The Evangelical Doctrine of Justification*. Grand Rapids, MI: Baker Book House, 1995

_____. *Getting the Gospel Right*. Grand Rapids, MI: Baker Book House, 1999

_____. *Grace Unknown: The Heart of Reformed Theology*. Grand Rapids, MI: Baker Book House, 2000

Stanley, Alan P. *Did Jesus Teach Salvation by Works?* Eugene, Ore: Pickwick *Publications,* 2006.

Stein, R.H. *Luke*. Vol. 24 of The New American Commentary. Nashville, TN: Broadman & Holman Publishers, 2001

Sturtz, Harry. *The Byzantine Text-Type and New Testament Textual Criticism*. Nashville, TN: Thomas Nelson, 1984

Thielman, Frank. *Theology of the New Testament*. Grand Rapids, MI: Zondervan, 2000

Tucker, Robert. *The Lenin Anthology*. Lenin, Vladimir. *One Step Forward, Two Steps Back (The Crisis in Our Party)*. New York: W. W. Norton and Company, 1975

VanLandingham, Chris. *Judgment & Justification in Early Judaism and the Apostle Paul*. Peabody, Mass: Hendrickson Publishers, Inc., 2006.

Wallace, Daniel. *Greek Grammar Beyond the Basics*. Grand Rapids, MI:
    Zondervan, 1996
_____. *The Basics of New Testament Syntax*. Grand Rapids, MI:
    Zondervan, 2000
Wegner, Paul. *A Student's Guide to Textual Criticism of the Bible*. Downers
    Grove, IL: InterVarsity Press, 2006
Witherington III, Ben. *Grace in Galatia* Grand Rapids, MI: Eerdmans, 1998
Zerwick, Max. *Biblical Greek Illustrated by Examples*. Rome: Pontificii
    Instituti Biblici, 1963.

Dictionaries/Encyclopedias:

Arndt, W., Danker, F. W., & Bauer, W. *A Greek-English lexicon of the New*
    Testament and other early Christian literature. "Based on Walter
    Bauer's Griechisch-deutsches Worterbuch zu den Schriften des
    Neuen Testaments und der frhüchristlichen [sic] Literatur, sixth
    edition, ed. Kurt Aland and Barbara Aland, with Viktor Reichmann
    and on previous English editions by W.F. Arndt, F.W. Gingrich,
    and F.W. Danker." 3rd ed. Chicago: University of Chicago Press,
    2000
Arndt, W., F. W. Gingrich, F. W. Danker, & W. Bauer. *A Greek-English*
    lexicon of the New Testament and other early Christian literature :
    A translation and adaptation of the fourth revised and augmented
    edition of Walter Bauer's Griechisch-deutsches Worterbuch zu den
    Schrift en des Neuen Testaments und der ubrigen urchristlichen
    Literatur. Chicago: University of Chicago Press, 1979
Balz, Horst and Gerhard Schneider, eds., *The Exegetical Dictionary of the*
    New Testament. Grand Rapids, MI; Eerdmans, 1991, s.v. G. Barth,
    "πίστις/ πιστεύειν, #4190"
Botterweck, G. Johannes and Helmer Ringgren, eds. *The Theological*
    Dictionary of the Old Testament. Vol. 1, rev. ed. Translated by John
    T. Willis. Grand Rapids, MI: Eerdmans, 1974, s.v. Alfred Jepsen,
    "אָמֵן"
Brown, Collin. *The New International Dictionary of New Testament*
    Theology. Vol. 1. Grand Rapids, MI: Zondervan, 1979, s.v. O.
    Becker, "Faith, Persuade, Belief, Unbelief"
Brown, Francis, Samuel Rolles Driver and Charles Augustus Briggs.
    Enhanced Brown-Driver-Briggs Hebrew and English Lexicon. Oak
    Harbor, WA: Logos Research Systems, 2000. CD-ROM. Logos
    Research System, Series X
Harris, R. Laird, Gleason Leonard Archer, and Bruce K. Waltke. *Theological*
    Wordbook of the Old Testament. Chicago: Moody Press, 1999
Kittel, Gerhard, Geoffrey William Bromley and Gerhard Friedrichs, eds. *The*
    Theological Dictionary of the New Testament. Grand Rapids, MI:
    Eerdmans, 1964-1976

Louw, J. P., & Nida, E. A. *Greek-English lexicon of the New Testament : Based on semantic domains*. New York: United Bible Societies; 1996

Moulton , J.H. and G. Milligan. *Vocabulary of the Greek Testament* Peabody, MA: Hendrickson Publishers, 1997

Swanson, James. *Dictionary of Biblical Languages With Semantic Domains : Hebrew (Old Testament)*, Oak Harbor, WA: Logos Research Systems, Inc., 1997. CD-ROM, Logos Bible Software, Series X

VanGemeren, William A. *The New international Dictionary of Old Testament Theology and Exegesis, Vol. 1* Grand Rapids, MI: Zondervan, 1997

Theses/Dissertations:

Bing, Charles C. "Lordship Salvation: A Biblical Evaluation and Response." Ph.D. diss.; Dallas Theological Seminary, 1991

Chay, Fred. "Lordship Salvation as Taught by John MacArthur." Th.M. diss.; Dallas Theological Seminary, 1983

_____. "A Strategy of Spiritual Motivation in the Book of Hebrews." D.Min. diss; Dallas Theological Seminary, 1990

_____. "A Textual and Theological Exposition on the Logion: The Salvation of the Soul." Ph.D. diss.; Trinity Theological Seminary, 2003

Pak, Joseph K. "A Study of Selected Passages on Distinguishing Marks of Genuine and False Believers." Ph.D. diss. Dallas Theological Seminary. 2001

Stuemann, Walter E. "A Critical Study of Calvin's Concept of Faith." Ph.D. diss.; University of Tulsa, 1952

Tracy, Steve. "Models of Faith Tested Against the Gospel of John." Th.M. diss.; Western Conservative Baptist Seminary, 1990

Uplinger, Wesly L. "The Problem of Confession in Romans 10:9-10." Th.M. thesis, Dallas Theological Seminary, 1968.

Journal Articles:

Aldrich, Roy. "The Gift of God." *Bibliotheca Sacra 122.* (July, 1965)

Anderson, David. "The Nature of Faith" *Chafer Theological Seminary Journal Volume 5.4* (September, 1999)

Bing, Charles C. "The Cost of Discipleship." *Journal of the Grace Evangelical Society Volume 6.* (Spring, 1993)

Blauvelt Jr., Livingston. "Does the Bible Teach Lordship Salvation?" *Bibliotheca Sacra 143.* (Jan, 1986)

Blue, J. Ronald. "Go, Missions" *Bibliotheca Sacra 141.* (October-December 1984)

Botha, J.E. "Pisteuo in the Greek New Testament: A Semantic-Lexicographical Study" *Neotestimentica 21*(1987)

Compton, R. Bruce. "James 2L21-24 and the Justification of Abraham." *Detroit Baptist Seminary Journal 2*. (Fall, 1997)

_____. "Persevering and Falling Away: A Reexamination of Hebrews 6:4-6." *Detroit Baptist Seminary Journal 1* (Spring, 1996)

Garlington, D.B. "The Obedience of Faith in the Letter to the Romans Part I: The meaning of ὑπακοὴ πίστεως (Rom 1:5; 16:26)." *Westminster Theological Journal 52:2* (Fall, 1990)

Gentry, Kenneth. "The Great Option: A Study of the Lordship Controversy." *Baptist Reformation Review 5* (Spring, 1976)

Hart, John F. "How to Energize our Faith: Reconsidering the Meaning of James 2:14-26." *Journal of the Grace Evangelical Society 12.* (Spring, 1999)

_____. "Why Confess Christ? The Use and Abuse of Romans 10:9-10." *Journal of the Grace Evangelical Society Volume 12:2.* (Autumn, 1999)

Hodges, Zane. "Light on James Two From Textual Criticism." *Bibliotheca Sacra 120.* (October, 1963)

_____. "Problem Passages in the Gospel of John Part II: Untrustworthy Believers-John 2:23-25." *Bibliotheca Sacra Volume 135* (April, 1978)

Hunn, Debbie. "The Believers Jesus Doubted." *Trinity Journal 25NS* (2004)

MacArthur, John. "Faith According to the Apostle James." *Journal of the Evangelical Theological Society 33.* (March, 1990.

Makidon, Michael. "Soteriological Concerns with Bauer's Greek Lexicon" *Journal of the Grace Evangelical Society vol. 17* (Autumn, 2004)

Niemelä, John. "Book Review of The Basics of New Testament Syntax: An Intermediate Greek Grammar: The Abridgement of 'Greek Grammar Beyond the Basics'" *Chafer Theological Seminary Journal 6:3* (July 2000)

_____. "Faith Without Works: A Definition." *Chafer Theological Seminary Journal 6.* (April, 2000)

_____. "James 2:24: Retranslation Required (Part 1 of 3)." *Chafer Theological Seminary Journal 7.* (January, 2001)

_____. "James 2:24: Retranslation Required Part 2 of 2." *Chafer Theological Seminary 7.* (April, 2001)

_____. "The Message of Life in the Gospel of John." *Chafer Theological Seminary Journal 7:3* (July, 2001)

Radmacher, Earl. "First Response to 'Faith According to the Apostle James' by John F. MacArthur, Jr." *Journal of the Evangelical Theological Society 33.* (March, 1990)

Rosscup, James E. "The Overcomer of the Apocalypse." *Grace Theological Journal Volume 3* (Fall, 1982)

Sapaugh, Gregory P. "Is Faith a Gift? A Study of Ephesians 2:8." *Journal of the Grace Evangelical Society.* (Spring, 1994)

Shepherd, Norman. *The Grace of Justification*, paper dated February 8, 1979, available on the Internet at: http://www.hornes.org/theologia/content/norman_shepherd/the_gra ce_of_justification.htm, 1979.

_____. *Thirty-four Theses on Justification in Relation to Faith, Repentance, and Good Works*, presented to the Presbytery of Philadelphia of the Orthodox Presbyterian Church, November 18, 1978, Available on the Internet at: http://www.hornes.org/theologia/content/norman_shepherd/the_34_ theses.htm, 1978.

Stagg, Frank. "The Abused Aorist." *Journal of Biblical Literature 91* (1972)

Turner, George Allen. "Soteriology in the Gospel of John." *Journal of the Evangelical Theological Society Volume 19* (Fall, 1976)

Unger, Merrill Frederick. "The Baptism with the Holy Spirit." *Bibliotheca Sacra 101:404* (October, 1944)

Wilkin, Robert. "Another View of Faith and Works in James 2." *Journal of the Grace Evangelical Society 15:2.* (Autumn 2002)

_____. "Repentance and Salvation Part 5: New Testament Repentance: Repentance in the Epistles and Revelation." *Journal of the Grace Evangelical Society 3:2* (Autumn, 1990)

_____. "A Review of R.C. Sproul's Grace Unknown: The Heart of Reformed Theology" *Journal of the Grace Evangelical Society volume 14:2* (August, 2001)

Biblical texts:

Biblia Hebraica Stuttgartensia : With Westminster Hebrew Morphology. Stuttgart; Glenside PA: German Bible Society; Westminster Seminary, 1996, c1925. Electronic ed. Oak Harbor, WA: Logos Research Systems, Inc., 1997. CD-ROM. Logos Bible Software, Series X.

Novum Testamentum Graece et Latine, apparatu critico instructum edidit Augustinus Merk S.J., editio octava, 1957.

Septuaginta : With morphology. Stuttgart: Deutsche Bibelgesellschaft, 1996, c1979. Electronic ed. Oak Harbor, WA: Logos Research Systems, Inc., 1997. CD-ROM. Logos Bible Software, Series X.

Aland, Barbara and Kurt, Johannes Karavidopoulos, Carlo M. Martini and Bruce Metzger, *Novum Testamentum Graece*. Stuttgart; German Bible Society, 1993

Aland, Barbara et. al., eds. *The Greek New Testament*, 4th ed. (UBS[4]). Stuttgart; The German Bible Society, 1998